DOCTOR McDOUGALL'S HEALTH-ENHANCING RECIPE BOOK

ISBN 1-56795-000-0

Book design by Kris Morgan.
Composition by Scribe Typography.
Illustration by Dave Albers.
Printed in the United States of America.

TABLE OF CONTENTS

INTRODUCTION

Mary McDougall has been inventing healthy recipes and testing them on her family and friends for more than sixteen years. With the help of her husband and unrestrained food critic, John, this book was compiled for you. Out of the 608 recipes found in *The McDougall Plan* and *The McDougall Health Supporting Cookbooks Volumes I and II,* over 100 of their personal favorites have been chosen.

One of the hardest steps for people new to healthy cooking is removing the fat from recipes. Helpful instructions for converting recipes to "oil-free" are provided. This book also contains information that would be hard to find in most other cookbooks on healthy cooking with beans, grains, and pastas.

One of the most useful sections of *The McDougall Program: 12 Days To Dynamic Health* is the list of "Acceptable Packaged and Canned Products" found on pages 100 to 114 and page 255. A list of newer products, updated September 1992, is provided for you in this book. Use these lists to find products in your grocery and natural food stores. If your store does not have the product you want, give the manager the information on the manufacturer from the list and ask him to order it. For further updates and more McDougall information, just mail a self-addressed stamped envelope to P.O. Box 14039, Santa Rosa, CA 95402.

With all the recipes provided and the packaged convenience products available, you could enjoy new dishes at every meal. However, most people soon discover and concentrate on their favorite choices. They have a few favorites for breakfast, a few for lunch, and for dinner they pick among a half dozen selections. If this sounds like you, then your task is to pick less than a dozen recipes you enjoy (or want to learn to enjoy) from the over 100 provided. Soon you will be creating your own healthful recipes that fit your tastes and needs perfectly.

Not every recipe is for every person. Some of you will have special dietary needs that must be addressed. For example, some of the recipes use high-fat plant foods—nuts, seeds, avocados, olives, and soybeans (tofu).

These richer recipes should be consumed in small amounts or on special occasions only by people who are already healthy and trim. The salt in some of these recipes would be hard on people who have experienced heart failure or have moderate to severe high blood pressure. Sugars found in fruits and fruit juices could keep triglycerides up in some sensitive people. The higher protein content of beans, peas, and lentils might be too much of a load on the kidneys for people who have had kidney failure. A few people are allergic to some of the vegetable foods. These susceptible people must identify the offending foods and avoid them.

Except for the very ill, most people tolerate small amounts of salt and sugar on the surface of their foods. You can also use your favorite spices liberally. With these three enjoyable substances and a touch of creativity, meals based around starches with the addition of vegetables and fruits will soon become your whole family's favorites. You'll give up nothing but poor health and a lifelong battle with obesity when you make this change.

Once people learn these principles of healthy eating, they do not turn back nor do they usually find a need to look for other solutions to their health and appearance problems. Some people, however, have a hard time following this prescription. If you find you are one, keep trying and realize learning is a process that sometimes takes years. Hopefully, you will become comfortable with your new eating habits soon (before a medical tragedy occurs), and join the thousands of people who have discovered that the secrets to good health and permanent weight control lie in their own hands.

Dietary and lifestyle changes are powerful medicine. Don't underestimate their potential impact. If you are ill or on medication, you should change your diet *only* under the supervision of a physician knowledgeable about the effects of foods and lifestyle on medication usage and disease. Read carefully those sections found in Part 3 of *The McDougall Program: 12 Days To Dynamic Health* that apply to your illness and discuss the information with your doctor. Your involvement in your recovery is essential for success. If you are willing to take this responsibility, you will likely experience healing, far greater than can be found with any medication or surgery, from the chronic diseases that plague people living in Western societies.

NEW ACCEPTABLE PACKAGED AND CANNED PRODUCTS

(Updated September, 1992)

Use with the list of "Acceptable Packaged and Canned Products" found on pages 100 to 114 and page 255 in *The McDougall Program: 12 Days To Dynamic Health*.

MANUFACTURER/DISTRIBUTOR	PRODUCT

Cold Cereals

Trader Joe's	Fat-Free Granola — Apple Strawberry
Alvarado St. Bakery	Organic Grinola
Health Valley	Fat-Free Granola
	Fiber 7 Flakes
Breadshop	Health Crunch
The Wheetabix Co.	Wheetabix Whole Wheat Cereal
	Grainfield's Raisin Bran

Hot Cereals

Pritikin Systems	Pritikin Hearty Hot Cereal—Apple Raisin Spice
Mercantile Food Co.	American Prairie Organic Hot Cereals
Lundberg Family Farms	Rice Cereal

Popcorn

Energy Food Factory	Poprice
Lapidus Popcorn Co.	Lite-Corn
Specialty Grain Co.	Pop-Lite Microwave Popcorn
Country Grown Foods	Gourmet Popcorn

Rice Cakes

Westbrae Natural Foods	Teriyaki Rice Cakes
Quaker Oats	Quaker Carmel Corn Cakes
Lundberg Family Farms	Organic Brown Rice Mini Rice Cakes

Crackers

Nabisco	Fat-Free Premium Crackers
Baja Bakery	Rice & Bean Tortilla Bites
Edwards & Sons Trading Co.	Brown Rice Sembei
Snack Cracks	Organic Rice Crackers—Tamari, Lightly Salted
Soken Products	Sesame Wheels—Brown Rice

Pretzels

J & J Snack foods	Super Pretzels—Frozen
Barbara's Bakery	Barbara's Whole Wheat Bavarian Pretzels

Chips

H.J. Heinz Co.	Weight Watchers Apple Chips
Guiltless Gourmet	Guiltless Gourmet No Oil Tortilla Chips
Barbara's Bakery	Basically Baked Organic Tortilla Chips
Trader Joe's	Baked Tortilla Chips
El Galindo Mexican Foods	Oil-Free Salted Baked Tortilla Chips, Oil-Free Blue Corn Baked Tortilla Chips

Breads

Great Harvest Bread Co.	Great Harvest Bakery—Honey Wheat, 9-Grain, Rye Onion, Dill, Country Whole Wheat
Brother Juniper's Bakery	Brother Juniper's Oil-Free Breads— Cajun Three Pepper, Oreganato, Whole Wheat
Alvarado St. Bakery	Alvarado St. Oil-Free Breads and Buns
Siljans Knacke	Siljans Knacke—Swedish Dark Rye Crispbread
Norganic Foods Co.	Katenbrot—Rye Bread
Ryvita	Ryvita Crisp Breads
Burns & Ricker	Crispini
Nokomis Farms	Country Loaf—Sourdough
Snack Cracks	Pizza Crust—Organic Brown Rice
Oasis Breads	Creative Crust Dinner Shells

| Trader Joe's | Force Primeval Bars—Raisin Walnut Apple Bars, Raisin Rolls Choyce |
| Health Valley | Fat-Free Muffins |

Soups

Dry Packaged:

Wil-Pak Foods	Taste Adventure Soups—Black Bean, Curry Lentil, Split Pea, Red Bean
Fantastic Foods	Fantastic Soups—Leapin Lentils Over Couscous, Fantastic Rockin' ABCs, Fantastic Jumpin Black Beans, Fantastic Splittin' Peas, Pinto Beans & Rice Mexicana
Nile Spice	Chili 'n Beans, Lentil, Black Bean, Split Pea
The Spice Hunter	Kasba Curry with Rice Bran, Mediterranean Minestrone

Canned:

Health Valley	Fat-Free Soups—5 Bean Vegetable, Country Corn and Vegetable, others
Westbrae	Ramen Express— Savory Szechaun, Oriental Vegetable, Golden Chinese; Noodles Anytime—Country Style
Hain Pure Food Co.	Fat-Free Soup—Vegetarian Split Pea, Vegetarian Veggie Broth
Mercantile Food Co.	American Prairie Vegetable Bean Soup
Trader Joe's	Mostly Unsplit Pea Soup

Burger Mixes/Meat Substitutes

Lima	Seitan (a wheat-derived "meat")
Santa Fe Organics	Hickory Smoked Seitan, others
Arrowhead Mills	Seitan, Quick Mix
Vegetarian Health Society	Vegetarian Hamburger Bits, Vegetarian Beef Chunks
Worthington Foods	GranBurger
Lightlife Foods	Smart Dogs (meatless hotdogs)

Egg-Free Pasta

Pastariso Products	Pastariso—Brown Rice Pasta
Food For Life Baking Co.	Wheat-Free Rice Elbows
Bertagni	Gnocchi di Palate
Eden Foods	Eden Vegetable Pastas
Food For Life Baking Co.	Rice Elbows

Bean and Vegetable Dishes *(frozen or refrigerated)*

Tumaro's	Black Bean Enchiladas
Amy's Kitchen	Amy's Organic Mexican Tamale Pie
United Foods	Pictsweet Express Microwaveable Vegetables
Bird's Eye, General Foods	Country Style Rice—Microwaveable

Dried Packaged Grains and Pastas

Arrowhead Mills	Wheat-Free Oatbran Muffin Mix , Griddle Lite Pancake & Baking Mix, Quick Brown Rice—Spanish Style, Vegetable Herb, Wild Rice & Herbs
Pritikin Systems	Pritikin Mexican Dinner Mix, Pritikin Brown Rice Pilaf
J.A. Sharwood & Co.	Sharwood's India Pilau Rice
Texmati Rice	Basmati Brown Rice
Sahara Natural Foods	Casbah Whole Wheat Couscous
Tipiak	Couscous
Nile Spice Foods	Whole Wheat Couscous, Couscous Salad Mix, Rozdali
Near East Food Products	Lentil Pilaf Mix
Liberty Imports	Instant Polenta
Jerusalem Natural Foods	Jerusalem Tabooleh
Aurora Import & Dist.	Polenta
Berhanu International Ltd.	Authentic Olde World—Lentils Divine

Salad Dressings

Pritikin Systems	Pritikin No-Oil Dressing (Ranch, Tomato, Italian, Russian, Creamy Italian, etc.)

Cook's Classics	Cook's Classic Oil-Free Dressings, (Country French, Garlic Gusto, Dijon, Dill)
St. Mary Glacier	St. Mary's Oil-Free Salad Dressing, (many flavors)
Trader Joe's	Trader Joe's—No-Oil Dill & Garlic Dressing, No-Oil Italian Dressing
Sweet Adelaide Enterprises	Paula's No-Oil Dressing
Nature's Harvest	Nature's Harvest—Oil-Free Vinaigrette, Oil-Free Herbal Splendor
Nakano USA	Seasoned Rice Vinegar
Uncle Grant's Foods	Uncle Grant's Salute—Honey Mustard Tarragon Dressing
S & W Fine Foods	Vintage Lites Oil-Free Dressing

Spaghetti Sauces

Campbell Soup Co.	Campbell's Healthy Request Marinara Sauce
S & W Fine Foods	Pasta Sauce
Pritikin Systems	Pritikin Spaghetti Sauce—Original, Chunky Garden Style
Hunt-Wesson	Healthy Choice Spaghetti Sauce
Nature's Harvest	Rocket Pesto
Tree of Life	Fat-Free Pasta Sauce
Sonoma Gourmet	Tomato Caper Herb Sauce

Soy Sauces

Edward & Sons Trading Co.	Ginger Tamari

Other Sauces

Lea & Perrins	Lea & Perrins Steak Sauce, HP Steak Sauce
San-J International	Teriyaki Sauce
Trader Joe's	Zucchini Relish
Reese Finer Foods	Old English Tavern Sauce
San-J International	Teriyaki Sauce

Salsa Sauces

Guiltless Gourmet	Guiltless Gourmet Picante Sauce
Pritikin Systems	Pritikin Salsa
Trader Joe's	Salsa Authentica, Salsa Verde
Nature's Harvest	Salsa

Baking Ingredients

Eden Foods	Eden Kuzu Root Starch, Agar Agar

Hot Drinks

J. Intra-World Grain Products	Café du Grain

Canned Bean and/or Vegetable Products

Brazos Products	Brazos Cajun Bean Dip
S&W Fine Foods	Maple Syrup Beans, Deli-Style Bean Salad, Mixed Bean Salad—bottled, Dill Garden Salad, Succotash, Garden Style Pasta Salad
Little Bear Organic Foods	Bearitos—Chili, Black Bean Dip
American Home Food Products	Salad Bar—Marinated Medley, Three Bean Salad, Garbanzo Beans, Kidney Beans
Del Monte Foods	Dennison's Chili Beans in Chili Gravy
Hunt-Wesson	Rosarita No Fat Refried Beans
Guiltless Gourmet	Bean Dips
Walnut Acres	Garbanzo Beans, Pinto Beans
Stop & Shop Supermarket Co.	Chick Peas
H.J. Heinz	Vegetarian Beans in Tomato Sauce
Trader Joe's	Spicy Black Bean Dip

Canned Tomato Products

Eden Foods	Crushed Tomatoes—No Salt Added
Trader Joe's	Tomato Sauce
S & W Fine Foods	No-Salt Added Ready-Cut Peeled Tomatoes
Ital Trade, U.S.A.	Pomi Strained Tomatoes, Pomi Chopped Tomatoes

| Walnut Acres | Tomato Purée, Tomatoes |

Canned Fruit Products

| Del Monte | Fruit Naturals—Diced Peaches, Mixed Fruit |

Acceptable Milks

Grainaissance	Amazake Rice Drink (now in paper cartons)
Sovex Natural foods	Better Than Milk? Light
Health Valley Foods	Low-Fat Soy Moo
	Fat-Free Soy Moo
Vitasoy U.S.A.	Vitasoy Light—Original 1%
Westbrae Natural Foods	West Soy Lite (1% Fat) Plain

RICHER FOODS

Cookies

Health Valley	Fat-Free Cookies—Raspberry, Raspberry Fruit Centers, Raisin Oatmeal, Apple Spice, others, Fat-Free Jumbo Fruit Bars—Apricot, Oat Bran, Raisin Cinnamon and others
Nature's Warehouse	Wheat-Free Cookies—Carmel Crisp, Raspberry
Heaven Scent Natural Foods	Cookies—Mountain Berry, Old-Fashioned Raisin
Auburn Farms	Fat-Free Jammers
R.W. Frookies	Fat-Free All Natural Cookies

Jellies, Jams, Syrups

Kozlowski Family	Apple Chutney, Fruit Jams
Lundberg Family Farms	Sweet Dreams Brown Rice Syrup
Timber Crest Farms	Dried Tomato Chutney
Nature's Harvest	Kiwi Preserve

Spring Tree Corp.	Pure Maple Syrup
Anderson's	Pure Maple Syrup
Camp	Pure Maple Syrup

Barbecue Sauces and Ketchups

| Beatrice/Hunt-Wesson | No Salt Added Tomato Ketchup |

Ice Desserts

| JM Smucker Co. | Fruitage Premium Frozen Dessert— Raspberry |

ACCEPTABLE HIGH-FAT TREATS

Soy Milks

Wholesome & Hearty	White Almond Beverage
Pacific Foods of Oregon	Organic Soy Beverage
Westbrae Natural Foods	Westsoy Plus

Soy Yogurt

| Soyen Natural | Soya Latté—Non-Dairy Yogurt |
| White Wave | White Wave Dairyless Yogurt |

Burger Mixes with Tofu

Fantastic Foods	Tofu Burger Mix, Tofu Scrambler Mix
Sunfield Foods	Lite Chef Country Barbecue
Sahara Natural Foods	Greek Classics—Gyros

Help us update this list. Please send identifying labels and/or packaging from products that help make eating healthy easier.

For an updated product list, send a self-addressed stamped envelope to:
McDougalls
P.O. Box 14039
Santa Rosa, CA 95402

HEALTHY COOKING TECHNIQUES

Cooking Without Oil

Cooking without oil does not mean cooking without flavor! Once you've begun to learn how easy it is to prepare delicious meals without oil, your opinion of oily foods will change. Oil is disgusting. No one would think of drinking a glass of olive or corn oil. People wash it off their dishes with strong detergents. The worst restaurants in town are unflatteringly referred to as "greasy spoons."

Yet almost all recipes use oil in one form or another as a prominent ingredient—unless they are from a McDougall book. You'll want to adapt your old favorites to the McDougall style. And, you'll be pleasantly surprised to discover that leaving out the oil will improve the taste of the food. However, you'll need to find ways to replace the moisture and other qualities oil used to provide. The following suggestions should help you make the transition to cooking without oil.

Sautéing Without Oil

To sauté implies the use of butter or oil. But McDougall cooking eliminates the oil and, instead, uses liquids that give taste without hazard to your health. Surprisingly, plain water makes an excellent sautéing liquid. It prevents foods from sticking to the pan but still allows vegetables to brown and cook, and it doesn't obscure the real flavor of the food.

For additional flavor, try sautéing in:

Soy sauce (Tamari)
Red or white wine (alcoholic or non-alcoholic)
Sherry (alcoholic or non-alcoholic)
Rice vinegar or balsamic vinegar
Tomato juice

Lemon or lime juice

Mexican salsa

Worcestershire sauce

For even more flavor, add herbs and spices, such as fresh grated ginger root, dry mustard, or fresh garlic along with any of the above.

BROWNING VEGETABLES

Browned onions develop a rich delicious flavor and can be used alone or mixed with other vegetables to create dishes with gourmet taste. To achieve the color of browning, as well as to add more flavor to your foods, place 1½ cups of chopped onions in a large nonstick frying pan with 1 cup of water. Cook over medium heat, stirring occasionally, until the liquid evaporates and the onions begin to stick to the bottom of the pan. Continue to stir for a minute, then add another ½ cup of water, loosening the browned bits from the bottom of the pan. Cook until the liquid evaporates again. Repeat this procedure 1 or 2 more times, until the onions (or mixed vegetables) are as browned as you like. You can also use this technique to brown carrots, green peppers, garlic, potatoes, shallots, zucchini, and many other vegetables, alone or mixed in a variety of delightful combinations.

BAKING WITHOUT OIL

You can eliminate oil in baking and still keep your baked goods moist and soft. Just replace the oil called for in the recipe with half the amount of another moist food, such as applesauce, mashed bananas, mashed potatoes, mashed pumpkin, tomato sauce, soft silken tofu, or soy yogurt (but remember: tofu and soy yogurt are high-fat foods).

Cakes and muffins made without oil are a little heavier. If you prefer a lighter texture, use carbonated water instead of tap water in baking recipes. Be sure to test cakes and muffins at the end of the baking time by inserting a toothpick or cake tester to see if it comes out clean. Sometimes oil-less cakes and muffins may need to be baked longer than the directions advise, depending on the weather or the altitude at which you live.

COOKING BASIC STARCHES

The more you know about starchy foods, the more likely you are to prepare meals cooked to perfection. Methods for boiling and steaming root vegetables like potatoes and yams, or squashes and green or yellow vegetables are simple and can be found in any cookbook. Cooking legumes, grains and pastas can be a little more difficult, mainly because many people are not familiar with all the varieties available.

COOKING LEGUMES

The legumes category includes a delightful array of beans, peas, and lentils. Inexpensive and easy to cook, they can be boiled on a stove top, simmered in a slow cooker, or prepared in a pressure cooker (except for soy beans, split peas and lentils). The most economical way to purchase legumes is in their dried state, in large bags holding from 5 to 100 pounds. They'll store well in a cool dry cupboard for months.

Before cooking, rinse and sort legumes by hand, removing stones and any beans that are discolored. Place legumes in a large pot in enough water to cover them, and bring to a boil. Reduce the heat, cover, and cook at a gentle boil for the recommended times listed below. The longer you cook legumes, the softer they become, the more their indigestible carbohydrates are broken down, and the less trouble you will have with bowel gas. Salads call for firmer beans cooked just to the point of being tender. Legumes for soups and spreads need to be cooked longer. Never add salt while cooking —it makes beans tough.

Cooking Times for Legumes

Beans (1 cup)	Water(cups)	Time(hours)	Yield(cups)
Adzuki Beans	4	1½	2
Black beans	4	1½	2
Black-eyed peas	3	1	2
Garbanzos	4	3	2
Kidney beans	3	2	2
Lentils★	3	1	2
Split peas★	3	1	2
Lima beans	3	1½	2
Pinto beans	3	2½	2
White beans	3	2	2

★Do not need pre-soaking.

In a hurry? Cooking times can be reduced by two methods:

1) Soak the beans overnight in enough water to cover them with 2 to 3 inches to spare. After soaking, drain off the water and cook according to instructions, but reduce the cooking time by 1 hour.

2) For another quicker preparation that saves both time and energy, bring the beans to a boil with the amount of water suggested above for 2 minutes, then remove them from the heat, cover, and let them rest for 1 hour. Do not drain. Then proceed with the directions given above, but reduce the cooking time by ½ hour.

If you use the longer cooking times in addition to these methods, you will end up with more thoroughly cooked, easily digestible beans.

Slow Cooking Legumes

Slow cookers are convenient, and they'll save you money on electricity. Just place the legumes in your slow cooker, cover with the amounts of water listed above, and cook for 6-8 hours on high, or 10-12 hours on low.

Pre-Cooked Legumes

Beans and lentils can be bought already cooked and packaged in bottles or cans. Black-eyed peas can be found cooked and frozen. As more people discover the delicious flavors and health benefits of legumes, more of these prepared foods will be found in the markets. The pre-cooked packaged varieties are more expensive, but more convenient. Their extra cost needs to be balanced against your savings in energy bills and against the value of your time.

Look for beans bottled or canned in water only or in water and salt. Drain and rinse the beans, then use them in any recipe calling for cooked beans, just as you would dried beans you cooked at home. In some recipes, however, you'll need to start with dried beans because their cooking liquid will become the basis of a sauce.

COOKING GRAINS

Rice is the most familiar grain to Americans and the most commonly consumed food in the world. Now, however, a wide variety of other whole grains are also available. Experiment with all of them. You will discover new favorite foods that rate high not only on the taste scale, but on the nutrition scale as well.

Boiling is the usual way to cook these grains. Bring the water to a boil in a saucepan. Slowly add the grain, return the water to a boil, cover, reduce the heat to low, and cook until the water has been absorbed. Do not stir. For a fluffier texture, allow the grain to rest uncovered for 15 minutes after cooking, then fluff with a fork. This helps dry the grain. For a delicious variation, try a mix of two or more grains, or use a vegetable stock instead of water.

Bulgur may also be prepared by pouring boiling water over it in a bowl. Cover the bowl with a kitchen towel and wait for 1 hour. Then pour the bulgur into a mesh strainer and press out any excess water.

Cooking Times for Grains

Whole grains (1 cup)	Water (cups)	Time (min.)	Yield (cups)
Barley	2	60	3
Buckwheat	2	15	2½
Bulgur wheat	2	15	2½
Cornmeal	4	30	3
Millet	3	45	3½
Quinoa	2	15	3
Rice (brown)	2	60	3
Rye	2	60	2½
Wheat berries	3	120	3

Grains can be cooked more easily and more reliably in a rice cooker. Unfortunately, most brands of rice cookers have aluminum insert bowls. To reduce contact of your grain with this possibly neurotoxic metal, use a stainless steel bowl inserted in the aluminum bowl. Better yet, National (made by Panasonic) and Hitachi manufacture rice cookers with a nonstick coating and stainless steel covers that protect your food from exposure to aluminum, and Trillium Health Products has just developed the Nutritionist,™ a multipurpose cooker with a nonstick coating and computer monitored cycles that ensure perfectly cooked rice, grains, and even grain/legume combinations.

5-Grain Recipe

2 cups brown rice

¼ cup barley

¼ cup millet

¼ cup wheat berries

¼ cup whole rye or wild rice

1 cup of this 5-Grain mixture should be cooked in 2 cups of water for 60 minutes.

COOKING PASTAS

Made from flour and water, pastas provide cholesterol-free, energy-packed meals. Wheat is the most common flour used, but often it's combined with other grain flours, so pastas offer a wide assortment of flavors and nutrients. For those who are wheat sensitive, some pastas are entirely wheat free, like those made from quinoa, corn, and rice.

Manufactured flours have lost some of their fiber in processing, and some of the more refined should be considered "white" flours. The 100% durum semolina pastas have the familiar flavor and body of "white" flour pastas. The flour with the highest content of dietary fiber is whole wheat flour, and you will notice this by the coarser texture of its pastas.

The most important consideration when choosing a pasta is to find one made of only flour and water, containing no eggs or oil. Good quality pasta makes a wonderful companion to simple, oil-free sauces.

Types of Pasta Flours

Artichoke pasta	Made from dehydrated artichoke flour and wheat flour

Buckwheat soba	Made from buckwheat flour and wheat flour
Corn pasta	Made from cornmeal and water
Quinoa	Made from corn, quinoa, and sesame flours
Rice	Made from ground brown rice
Soy pasta	Made from soy flour and wheat flour
Spinach pasta	Made from ground dehydrated spinach and wheat flour
Tomato pasta	Made from ground dehydrated tomatoes and wheat flour
Whole wheat pasta	Made from whole wheat flour

Pasta Shapes

Conchiglie rigate	Large or small pasta shells
Cannelloni	Large pasta tubes
Farfalle	Bow or butterfly shaped pasta
Fettuccini	Long flat strands
Fusilli	Spirals, in a variety of widths and lengths
Lasagne	Large flat pasta, with frilled edges
Linguine	Thin flat strands
Macaroni	Narrow tubes, usually curved, in a variety of lengths
Penne ziti	Quill-shaped tubes, ridged or plain
Rigatoni	Wide ridged tubes
Spaghetti	Long thin round strands
Vermicelli	Long thin threads

To cook 1 pound of pasta, you'll need about four to five quarts of water. Do not add oil or salt to the water. One pound of pasta will serve four people with normal appetites. Bring the water to a rolling boil. Drop the pasta into the water. (It's not necessary to break long strands; they'll soften and sink into the water.) Cook the pasta uncovered at a rolling boil, and stir it occasionally. After 5 minutes, test the pasta for readiness by biting into a piece. Pasta should be firm, or *al dente*, never soggy. Cooking time will vary, but should take no longer than 12 minutes. When the pasta is done, drain it in a colander, rinse with cool water to help prevent sticking, then put it in a bowl. Serve immediately or mix with sauce before serving. Mixing with a sauce not only adds flavor, it keeps the strands of pasta from sticking together as they cool.

SEASONING FOODS

You may prefer to add more or less spice than the recipes call for. Use recipes as guidelines only. Particular combinations of spices produce flavors identified with certain types of ethnic dishes. Take advantage of these spice combinations to vary recipes and create new ones.

Mexican	Italian	Asian	Greek	Indian
Salsa	Parsley	Soy sauce	Lemon juice	Tumeric
Chili powder	Basil	Ginger	Cinnamon	Pepper
Cumin	Oregano	Dry mustard	Cumin	Cilantro
Cilantro	Garlic	Garlic	Pepper	Cumin

SALT AND SUGAR

Taste buds for salt and sugar are found on the tip of the tongue. It appears we are designed to seek both of these pleasurable tastes. If salt and sugar are used in reasonable amounts, most healthy people will be able to enjoy both substances without ill effects.

Salt is the taste missed most when people switch to a healthful diet. If you feel the food is bland, salt is what you are missing. Sugar can also do wonders for making food palatable. Some health problems may restrict one substance (for example, high blood pressure may restrict use of salt), but not the other (sugar). By using whichever has no ill effects for you, or if neither is a problem, balancing the use of these ingredients, you will end up with very enjoyable meals.

Use salt and/or sugar on the surface of your foods rather than letting them be absorbed during cooking. This direct contact provides your taste buds with the greatest stimulation for the least amount of substance.

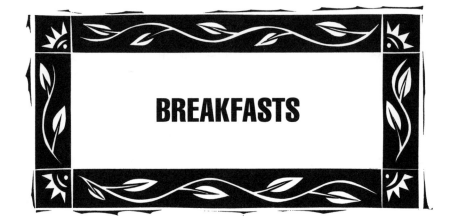

BREAKFASTS

CASHEW FRENCH TOAST

Yield: 16 slices Preparation Time: 10 minutes
Cooking Time: 15 minutes

You'll wonder what the eggs are for in your old French toast recipe once you try this cholesterol-free version, made extra rich by the use of cashews. Children love it!

½ cup raw cashews	⅛ teaspoon cinnamon
2¼ cups water	dash turmeric
3 tablespoons chopped dates	16 slices whole wheat bread

Place all ingredients (except the bread) into a blender jar. Blend thoroughly until smooth. Pour into a bowl. Dip slices of bread into cashew mixture, coating both sides. Brown on a medium-hot, nonstick griddle, turning once so both sides are evenly browned. Serve plain, with fruit sauces, or with pure maple syrup.

Helpful Hints: This recipe can easily be doubled. The toast freezes very nicely if individually wrapped and can be popped into the toaster for a quick, delicious breakfast.

BANANA PANCAKES

Yield: 12 pancakes Preparation Time: 10 minutes
Cooking Time: 15 minutes

A reporter in the cooking section of our local newspaper said she made these every morning for her husband—and he loved them.

1 cup whole wheat pastry flour

2 teaspoons baking powder

1¼ cups nut milk, rice milk or fruit juice

2 tablespoons unsweetened applesauce

1 medium size, firm but ripe banana, finely chopped

Mix the flour and baking powder together. Mix the liquid with the applesauce, and add to the dry ingredients. Stir until just moistened. Fold in the banana. Drop the batter by spoonfuls onto a hot nonstick griddle. Turn the pancakes when bubbles appear; brown the other side.

APPETIZERS

GARBANZO PURÉE

Yield: 2 cups   Preparation Time: 15 minutes
Cooking Time: 3 hours

This has been a long-time favorite dip in our family. It's very similar to hummus, but without all the fat you'd get from the tahini.

3 cups cooked garbanzo beans

1 tablespoon lemon juice

¼ teaspoon basil

¼ teaspoon garlic powder

1 teaspoon onion powder

½ teaspoon ground cumin

1 tablespoon parsley flakes

Purée the beans, then mix all of the ingredients together. (This can be done in a blender.) Also, some water or bean-cooking liquid may be added to produce a creamier consistency.

Let stand an hour at room temperature to blend flavors.

Use as sandwich spread, to fill pocket bread (also called pita bread), or as a dip for crackers or fresh vegetables.

MARINATED MUSHROOMS

Servings: 6-10   Preparation Time: 15 minutes
Chilling Time: 2-3 hours

A great appetizer to bring to a party. Be sure to make plenty—they'll go fast!

1 pound bite-sized mushrooms

2 green peppers, cut into ¾-inch pieces

1 small onion, cut into wedges and then separated

1 cup water

1 cup red wine vinegar

1 tablespoon honey

2 teaspoons dry mustard

2 teaspoons low-sodium soy sauce

Prepare mushrooms by rinsing and trimming stems. Set them aside in a bowl with the green pepper and onions. In a pan, combine the water, vinegar, honey, mustard, and soy sauce. Bring to a boil. Pour over the mushrooms, green peppers, and onions. Cover. Marinate in the refrigerator for several hours.

Before serving, thread on small bamboo skewers.

LENTIL-MUSHROOM PÂTÉ

Yield: about 4 cups   Preparation Time: 15 minutes
Cooking Time: 50 minutes

A very rich and flavorful spread, the strong flavor of this pâté makes it my favorite cracker and sandwich topping. The recipe was created by one of our best friends in Hawaii and it makes a lot. It freezes well if not all used immediately.

1 cup lentils	1 teaspoon sage
4 cups water	1 teaspoon thyme
½ pound mushrooms, sliced	1 teaspoon dry mustard
1 onion, chopped	½ teaspoon cayenne pepper
1 clove garlic, crushed	¼ teaspoon black pepper
1 tablespoon parsley flakes	¼ teaspoon allspice
1 teaspoon basil	¼ teaspoon ground ginger
1 teaspoon chervil	1 bay leaf
1 teaspoon marjoram	2 tablespoons low-sodium soy sauce
1 teaspoon rosemary	1 tablespoon sherry

Cook lentils in water until tender (about 40 minutes), then drain them in a strainer. While the lentils are cooking, sauté the onion and garlic in ¼ cup water over medium heat for 5 minutes. Add the mushrooms and sauté 5 minutes longer. Add the herbs and spices and continue to cook for 10 more minutes, adding more water as needed. Add the soy sauce, sherry, and drained lentils. Cook until the liquid is absorbed and the mixture starts to stick to the pan. Take the pan from the heat, remove the bay leaf, and purée the mixture in a food processor or blender until smooth. Serve warm or chilled.

Serve with triangles of whole wheat toast. Also delicious spread on thin, crisp rye crackers.

STUFFED MUSHROOM CAPS

Servings: 6-10 Preparation Time: 40 minutes
Cooking Time: 15 minutes

Great party food—this recipe will be a hit even with people who never thought they'd like anything that came out of a book by McDougall! The tofu makes this recipe higher in fat, so save for festive occasions.

38-40 medium large mushrooms (or 20-22 extra large size)

1 (10-ounce) package frozen chopped spinach

1 package dehydrated onion soup mix (such as Hain)

1½ cups soft blended tofu

½ teaspoon garlic powder (optional)

Thaw the spinach and press out any liquid. Clean the mushrooms, remove and discard their stems, and arrange them on a nonstick baking sheet, bottom side up. Combine soup mix, tofu, garlic powder, and thawed spinach. Mix well.

Place a small amount of the spinach-tofu mixture into each mushroom cap and flatten slightly. Repeat until all are filled.

Bake, covered, in a 350°F oven for 15 minutes. Serve hot.

Helpful Hints: The mushrooms may be made ahead of time, then refrigerated until baking. If you can't find large mushrooms, use medium ones. You will need to buy a few more in that case. Check after cooking 12 minutes. Sometimes smaller mushrooms cook faster. Many "natural" onion soup mixes are now on the market. Look for ones that do not contain oil. For a variation, try using Tofu Mayonnaise or Dijon Tofu Dip instead of plain blended tofu.

SOUPS

ORIENTAL VEGETABLE SOUP

Servings: 4-8 Preparation Time: 30 minutes
Cooking Time: 30 minutes

I developed this recipe as I learned about the delicious cuisine of the Orient while living in Hawaii. My Oriental Vegetable Soup is a healthy version of Saimin, which is such a favorite in Hawaii that it's served at McDonalds!

10 cups water	2 packages dried shiitake mushrooms
1½ cups mushroom liquid	1 onion, cut in wedges
¼ cup low-sodium soy sauce	1 bunch green onions, cut in 1-inch pieces
¼ cup sherry (optional)	3 stalks celery, sliced
2-3 garlic cloves, crushed	½ pound Chinese cabbage, sliced
1 tablespoon grated fresh ginger	½ pound buckwheat soba noodles

Place mushrooms in mixing bowl. Pour 2 cups of hot water over the mushrooms and let soak for 15 minutes.

Meanwhile, put 10 cups of water in a large soup pot. Add the soy sauce, sherry, ginger, and garlic. Bring to a boil. Add the onion wedges. Reduce the heat.

Squeeze excess water from the mushrooms, reserving the liquid. Add 1½ cups of this liquid to the hot broth. Chop the mushrooms, discarding the tough stems, and add to the broth. Add the remaining ingredients, except the noodles.

Simmer over low heat 15 minutes, then add noodles and cook an additional 10 minutes. Serve hot.

Helpful Hints: This will make a meal for four people, or a first course for eight people.

BARLEY SOUP

Servings: 6-8 Preparation Time: 20 minutes
Cooking Time: 2 hours

This is my healthy version of a cabbage-barley soup served at some Big Boy's Restaurants in Detroit, Michigan.

8 cups water

¾ cup barley

2 teaspoons dill weed

1 teaspoon cumin (optional)

1 large onion, chopped

½ pound mushrooms, sliced

1 pound cabbage, coarsely chopped

2 tablespoons chopped parsley

1 bay leaf

Put the barley, water, onions and seasonings in a large pot. Cover and simmer about 2 hours. For the last 30 minutes of cooking time, add the mushrooms and cabbage. Add more water if necessary.

CURRIED PEA SOUP

Servings: 6 Preparation Time: 30 minutes
Cooking Time: 2 hours

My favorite pea soup! And it will be yours too if you enjoy curry. I make this just for myself sometimes when my family is having a less spicy soup.

2 cups dried split peas	1 onion, grated
10 cups water	½ teaspoon celery seed
1 carrot, grated	½ teaspoon curry powder
2 potatoes, grated	2 cups brown rice, cooked

Place split peas in a large soup pot with 10 cups of water. Bring to a boil, then cover and cook over low heat about 1 hour. Meanwhile, grate the vegetables.

After peas have cooked about 1 hour, add the grated vegetables, celery seed, and curry powder. Cover and cook for 30 minutes. Add the cooked rice. Cook about 30 minutes more before serving.

WHITE BEAN SOUP

Servings: 6 Preparation Time: 15 minutes
Cooking Time: 3-4 hours

John's and the children's favorite soup. Be sure to presoak, drain, and rinse the beans to remove hard to digest sugars; otherwise, watch out for beans' familiar after-effect!

2 cups navy beans or Great Northern beans	2 bay leaves
8 cups water	½ teaspoon sage
2 onions, chopped	½ teaspoon oregano
2 stalks celery, chopped	1 tablespoon low-sodium soy sauce

Place the beans in 8 cups of water in a large pot. Bring to a boil, then remove from heat and let rest 1 hour. Add onions, celery, and seasonings. Simmer over low heat, covered, about 3 hours.

Helpful Hints: Cook this soup in a slow cooker, setting the timer for about 8 hours on high or 10-12 hours on low. For a thicker, creamier version, place 2-3 cups of the soup in a blender. Blend until smooth. Return to the soup pot and mix in well. This soup makes a flavorful, protein-rich sandwich spread when cold.

MILD GAZPACHO

Servings: 4 Preparation Time: 20 minutes
Chilling Time: 2 hours

Try this soup as a salad dressing or a delicious cold drink. Or serve gazpacho with a salad on those summer nights when it's too hot to cook.

4 cups tomato juice	2 celery stalks
2 tomatoes	½ cup fresh parsley
1 green pepper	1 teaspoon basil
1 cucumber	juice of ½ lemon
2 green onions	1 tablespoon low-sodium soy sauce

Cut the vegetables in large chunks to make blending easier. Put 2 cups of the tomato juice in blender along with half of the vegetables. Blend well. Pour into a large jar. Repeat with the remaining tomato juice, parsley, basil, lemon juice, and soy sauce. Blend. Add to the first batch. Mix well. Cover and chill at least 2 hours to blend flavors. Serve cold.

LENTIL SOUP

Servings: 8-10 Preparation Time: 30 minutes
Cooking Time: 60 minutes

This is the first lentil soup recipe I developed back in the '70s and it's still my favorite.

2 cups uncooked lentils	2 small potatoes, chopped
10 cups water	⅓ cup barley
2 carrots, sliced	2 tablespoons parsley flakes
1 celery stalk, chopped	2 bay leaves
2 onions, chopped	2 teaspoons cumin

Combine all the ingredients in a soup pot and cook until the lentils are soft, about 1 hour. Remove bay leaves before serving.

Helpful Hints: Brown rice may be substituted for the barley. This soup freezes well; save some for a busy day.

HOT YAM SOUP

Servings: 8 Preparation Time: 30 minutes
Cooking Time: 30 minutes

Be adventursome—I promise you'll really enjoy this richly colored, richly flavored soup.

2 onions, sliced

2 cloves garlic, crushed

2 stalks celery, chopped

1 cup chopped green beans

2 cups chopped peeled yams (or sweet potatoes or winter squash)

5½ cups water

1½ cups cooked garbanzo beans (optional)

1 large tomato, chopped

2 tablespoons low-sodium soy sauce

1 bay leaf

3 teaspoons paprika

1½ teaspoons tumeric

1½ teaspoons basil

⅛ teaspoon cinnamon

⅛ teaspoon Tabasco™ sauce (optional)

Place onions, garlic, celery, green beans, and yams in a large soup pot with ½ cup water. Cook over medium heat about 5 minutes. Stir occasionally. Add the remaining ingredients. Bring to a boil, reduce heat, cover, and simmer over low heat for 20 minutes.

Helpful Hints: If you don't have any green beans, try a cup of peas or chopped green pepper.

SUMMERTIME CHOWDER

Servings: 6-8 Preparation Time: 30 minutes
Cooking Time: 45 minutes

This soup uses many of the delicious vegetables you'll find fresh in summer. Its white color will leave everyone wondering how you made it without a drop of cow's milk.

1 onion, chopped	3 cups water
1 clove garlic, pressed	3 tablespoons low-sodium soy sauce
2 stalks celery, thinly sliced	2 teaspoons basil
2 carrots, thinly sliced	½ teaspoon white pepper
2 potatoes, peeled and diced	3 cups rice milk or nut milk
4 ears corn on the cob	chopped parsley or alfalfa sprouts (optional)
3 tomatoes, seeded and chopped	

In a large soup pot, sauté onion, garlic, celery, and carrot in ⅓ cup water about 10 minutes.

While this is cooking, remove corn from cob using a sharp knife. With the back of the knife, scrape the cob to extract creamy pulp. Reserve corn and pulp. (Should be about 2 cups.)

Add 3 cups water, potatoes, and seasonings to the soup pot. Bring to a boil. Add the corn and pulp. Mix well, reduce heat, cover, and cook about 15 minutes.

Add tomatoes and cook an additional 10-15 minutes.

Add 3 cups rice or nut milk, heat through and serve at once. Garnish with chopped parsley or alfalfa sprouts, if desired.

Helpful Hints: Tomatoes are added later in the cooking to prevent them from getting too mushy. Frozen corn could be used in place of fresh corn, if desired. Use about 2 cups. The white pepper makes this a very spicy soup; reduce to ¼ teaspoon for less spiciness.

FRENCH PEASANT SOUP

Servings: 6-8   Preparation Time: 20 minutes
Cooking Time: 1½ hours

This is a simple hearty peasant soup. It can also be served over potatoes, stuffed in pita bread or rolled up in chapatis. It even makes a delicious sandwich spread when cold.

8 cups water

1 cup dried lima beans

½ cup dried yellow split peas

1 cup bulgur wheat

1 large onion, chopped

2 cloves garlic, crushed

3 cups chopped cabbage

3 cups winter squash, peeled and chopped

2 potatoes, chopped

1 (16-ounce) can tomatoes, chopped

3 tablespoons low-sodium soy sauce

½ teaspoon crushed red pepper

½ teaspoon tarragon

½ teaspoon chervil

¼ teaspoon marjoram

¼ teaspoon thyme

1 tablespoon parsley flakes

Place water in a large soup pot. Add lima beans and cook over medium heat for 30 minutes. Add remaining ingredients. Cook an additional 60 minutes.

MANHATTAN BEAN SOUP

Servings: 8 Preparation Time: 30 minutes
Cooking Time: 3 hours

This soup has the rich tomato-y color and texture of Manhattan Clam Chowder, but it's so much healthier for you!

7 cups water

1 cup Great Northern beans

½ cup baby lima beans

1 onion, chopped

1 stalk celery, chopped

1 large potato, chopped

1 (16-ounce) can chopped tomatoes

2 tablespoons low-sodium soy sauce

¼ teaspoon ground coriander

¼ teaspoon dry mustard

dash white pepper

1½ cups non-dairy milk (rice, oat, nut, soy)

Place the beans and water in a soup pot. Bring to a boil, reduce the heat, cover and cook about 2 hours. Add vegetables and seasonings. Cook an additional hour. Remove 1 cup of soup and process in your blender until smooth. Add the milk to the blended soup and mix well. Add the blended mixture back to soup pan. Stir until heated through.

MEXICAN BEAN SOUP

Servings: 6 Preparation Time: 15 minutes
Cooking Time: 3 hours

The chili powder and cumin make this soup an instant hit with anyone who likes Mexican foods. Originally, I created this recipe for my oldest son because he loves pinto beans in any form.

2 cups pinto beans	½ teaspoon ground oregano
8 cups water	½ teaspoon ground cumin
1 large onion, chopped	2 tablespoons low-sodium soy sauce (optional)
2 teaspoons chili powder	dash or two of Tabasco™ (optional)

Place beans and water in a large soup pot. Bring to a boil, reduce heat, cover and cook over medium-low heat for 1 hour. Add remaining ingredients and continue to cook for about 2 hours, until beans are tender.

Helpful Hints: This soup can be made in a slow cooker. Just add all ingredients at once, and cook on high for about 6-8 hours.

GOURMET ONION SOUP

Servings: 6-8 Preparation Time: 25 minutes
Cooking Time: 60 minutes

An onion lover's delight. And since the onions are thoroughly cooked, it's easy on the stomach.

2 onions, sliced into rings	2 teaspoons whole wheat flour
2 leeks, sliced (white and light green parts)	7 cups water
12 green onions, sliced	1 cup white wine (or use water)
¼ cup minced shallots	¼ cup low-sodium soy sauce
2 cloves garlic, crushed	1 teaspoon lemon juice
2 teaspoons grated fresh ginger root	fresh ground pepper
pinch cayenne pepper	fresh chives, snipped

Sauté onions in ½ cup water for 5 minutes. Add leeks, green onions, and shallots with another ½ cup water. Sauté a few minutes to soften. Add garlic, ginger, and cayenne. Stir a few times, then add flour and stir for several minutes to thoroughly blend in. Slowly mix in water, wine, and soy sauce. Bring to boil, reduce heat, cover, and simmer for 45 minutes.

Add lemon juice and several twists of ground pepper. Mix. Ladle into bowls and garnish with snipped chives.

SPANISH GARBANZO SOUP

Servings: 8-10 Preparation Time: 20 minutes
Cooking Time: 3 hours

The combination of garbanzo beans and artichokes make this a European rather than a Latin-American soup. Its mild spices flavor it just enough to be interesting, but not so much that those who prefer less spicy food won't also enjoy it.

2 cups garbanzo beans

10 cups water

⅓ cup brown rice

1 (16-ounce) can tomatoes

2 onions, chopped

1 green pepper, chopped

2 cloves garlic, crushed

1 teaspoon chili powder

½ teaspoon oregano

½ teaspoon ground cumin

pinch powdered saffron (optional)

black pepper (optional)

2 tablespoons low-sodium soy sauce

1 (14-ounce) can artichoke hearts (water packed and drained)

Cook the garbanzos in the water for 2 hours. Then add the remaining ingredients, except the artichokes, and cook an additional hour. Add the artichokes after 45 minutes and continue to cook 15 minutes longer.

Helpful Hints: Reheats well.

HEARTY VEGETABLE SOUP

Servings: 10-12 Preparation Time: 30-40 minutes
Cooking Time: 1½ hours

You'll find this an excellent one pot meal. Just serve with your favorite bread to satisfy the heartiest appetite.

4 onions, chopped

3 cloves garlic, pressed

2 green peppers, chopped

1 cup water

1 teaspoon basil

1 teaspoon oregano

1 teaspoon ground cumin

1 tablespoon chili powder

4 cups chopped, canned tomatoes and their juice

1 cup tomato sauce

4 cups water

1 cup red wine (optional)

3 medium potatoes, cut in chunks

3 medium carrots, sliced

1 cup green beans

1 cup corn kernels

1 cup whole grains, cooked

1 ½ cups beans (pinto, kidney, garbanzo, white), cooked

2 cups leafy greens (kale, spinach, collards, etc.), shredded

Garnishes: chopped green onions, chopped parsley, chopped chives

Using a large soup pot, sauté the onions, garlic and green pepper in 1 cup water for 5 minutes. Add the spices, stir, and cook a few more minutes. Add tomatoes, tomato sauce, additional water, and the wine, if desired. Also add some fresh ground black pepper, if desired. Cover and cook over medium heat about 15 minutes to blend flavors. Add potatoes and carrots, cook for 30 minutes. Add green beans and corn, cook for 15 minutes. Add cooked grains and beans, plus greens. Cook an additional 15 minutes. Garnish with chopped parsley, chives or green onions just before serving.

Helpful Hints: This recipe makes a large amount but freezes well. Or, reduce the amount of each ingredient by half for 5-6 servings. Try omitting some of the vegetables and/or substituting other vegetables.

COUNTRY VEGETABLE SOUP

Servings: 6-8 Preparation Time: 35 minutes
Cooking Time: 1 to 1½ hours

This recipe originally came from the Outrigger Canoe Club (Tom Selleck was a member, but I don't know if he liked the soup).

1 cup dried red beans	3 cloves garlic, chopped
1 cup dried garbanzo beans	3 whole tomatoes, skinned and chopped
2 medium potatoes, thinly sliced	2 bay leaves
2 leeks, thinly sliced	2 whole cloves
2 medium onions, thinly sliced	1 pinch thyme
1 carrot, thinly sliced	1 pinch marjoram
3 celery ribs, thinly sliced	white pepper (optional)
1 small turnip, thinly sliced	chopped parsley or basil (optional)

Soak beans separately overnight in 1 quart water each. Cook beans separately in their soaking liquids. Each will take approximately 1 to 1½ hours to cook.

Place the remaining ingredients in a large soup pot with 2½ quarts of water. Bring to a boil, cover, reduce the heat and simmer for 1 hour. Add cooked beans. Heat through. Remove cloves and bay leaves. Garnish with chopped fresh parsley or sweet basil before serving.

SOUTH OF THE BORDER SOUP

Servings: 8 Preparation Time: 30 minutes
Cooking Time: 60 minutes

A soup with real Mexican flavor and a special favorite of those who don't care for beans.

6 cups water

1½ cups Picante sauce

2 cloves garlic, crushed

2 onions, cut into wedges

5 carrots, sliced ½ inch thick

4 medium potatoes, cut into large chunks

½ cup long grain brown rice

1 green pepper, cut into ½-inch pieces

1 rib celery, cut into ½-inch slices

½ small cabbage, shredded

2 cups corn kernels

2 tomatoes, cut into wedges

fresh chopped cilantro (optional)

2 lemons, cut into wedges (optional)

Place the 6 cups of water in a large soup pot. Add the picante sauce (either mild, medium, or hot depending on your taste buds). Add the garlic, onions, carrots, potatoes, and rice. Cook over medium heat for 30 minutes. Add the green pepper, celery, cabbage, and corn. Cook 20 minutes longer. Add the tomatoes and cilantro (if desired), and heat through. Serve in large bowls. Garnish with lemon wedges, if desired. Pass more warmed picante sauce to spoon on at the table.

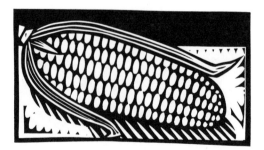

MUSHROOM SOUP

Servings: 6 Preparation Time: 15 minutes
Cooking Time: 30 minutes

A fast, easy soup that's a real favorite for mushroom lovers. Try using your favorite types of exotic mushrooms for a gourmet treat.

1½ pounds mushrooms, sliced

1 onion, thinly sliced

1 large clove garlic, crushed

2 bay leaves

¾ cup white wine (or apple juice)

5 cups water

3 to 4 tablespoons low-sodium soy sauce

1 teaspoon honey

1½ teaspoons basil

2 teaspoons dill weed

1 teaspoon paprika

freshly ground black pepper

Combine all ingredients in large saucepan. Bring to a boil, reduce heat, cover, and simmer for about 30 minutes.

GREEN ONION SOUP

Servings: 6 Preparation Time: 20 minutes
Cooking Time: 30 minutes

A delicate soup that's not too filling. Perfect to whet the appetite as a first course.

6 large leeks	⅛ teaspoon white pepper
6 ½ cups water	3 cups green onions, including tops, thinly sliced
2½ tablespoons whole wheat flour	½ cup white wine (optional)
⅛ teaspoon sage	1 tablespoon lemon juice
⅛ teaspoon oregano	dash or two of Tabasco™
½ teaspoon parsley flakes	fresh lemon slices (optional)
2 tablespoons low-sodium soy sauce	

Prepare the leeks by cutting off root ends and tough green stems. Split the leeks lengthwise and rinse them out well. Thinly slice and rinse again if necessary.

Place the leeks in a large pot with ½ cup water. Cook and stir over medium heat until the leeks are very soft, about 20 minutes. Add more water if necessary. Stir in the flour. Add the remaining water and spices. Bring to a boil, add the green onions and wine (if desired). Cook 5 minutes. Stir in lemon juice and Tabasco. Serve garnished with fresh lemon slices.

POTATO CHOWDER

Servings: 10 Preparation Time: 30 minutes
Cooking Time: 55 minutes

A soup passed along as a tradition in the Irish McDougall clan.

1 large onion, coarsely chopped

3 stalks celery, sliced

1 green pepper, chopped

2 carrots, sliced

2 cloves garlic, crushed

6½ cups water

4 large potatoes, cubed

2 tablespoons low-sodium soy sauce

1 teaspoon basil

½ teaspoon paprika

¼ teaspoon pepper

1 (28-ounce) can chopped tomatoes in their juice

Place the chopped onion, celery, green pepper, carrots, and garlic in a large soup pot with ½ cup water. Sauté for 5 minutes, until the vegetables are crisp-tender. Add the potatoes, soy sauce, basil, paprika, pepper, and remaining water. Bring to a boil, reduce heat, cover, and cook over medium-low heat for 30 minutes. Add the tomatoes, cover, and cook an additional 20 minutes.

SALADS

TABOULI

Servings: 3-4 Preparation Time: 1 hour to soak bulgur;
15 minutes to mix Chilling Time: 2 hours

A great make-ahead dish, easy to take to a pot-luck, dinner, or picnic. Try it stuffed in pita bread for a different sandwich idea. This recipe can be doubled or quadrupled easily for larger amounts. Keeps well in refrigerator.

½ cup dry bulgur wheat

1 cup boiling water

¼ cup chopped green onions (about 3)

1 tomato, chopped

½ cup garbanzo beans, cooked

½ cup fresh parsley, chopped

¼ cup fresh mint, chopped

2 tablespoons lemon juice

⅛ teaspoon garlic powder

Put the bulgur in a small mixing bowl. Pour the boiling water over the bulgur. Mix. Cover with a towel and let stand for 1 hour. After 1 hour, the excess water should be removed. The easiest way to do this is to pour the bulgur and water into a fine mesh strainer. Let the water drain off, pressing the bulgur with your hands to remove as much of the excess water as possible. Place the drained bulgur in a bowl. Add the remaining ingredients. Toss well to mix. Cover and refrigerate at least 2 hours to blend flavors.

RICE SUMMER SALAD

Servings: 6-8 Preparation Time: 30 minutes
Chilling Time: 2 hours

Serve as a cool main dish for a hot summer evening, either plain or piled on lettuce leaves and garnished with tomatoes and watercress.

4 cups cooked, long-grain brown rice	1 large green pepper, chopped
½ cup cider or wine vinegar	1 large tomato, chopped
¼ teaspoon dry mustard	1 cup cooked green peas
1 teaspoon tarragon	4-5 tablespoons diced pimento
6 green onions, finely chopped	¼ cup chopped parsley
2 stalks celery, chopped	1 cucumber, chopped (optional)

Mix the vinegar, mustard, and tarragon. Pour over the cooked rice. If the rice is warm, let it cool to room temperature before adding remaining ingredients. Mix well. Toss gently. Cover and refrigerate at least 2 hours before serving.

Helpful Hints: For a variation, substitute basil or dill weed for the tarragon. Short-grain brown rice can also be used.

CARROT ORANGE SALAD

Servings: 6 Preparation Time: 15 minutes
Chilling Time: 2 hours

A healthier version of the traditional favorite served at restaurant salad bars. Vary the sweetness to your taste by changing the amounts of honey and juices used.

¾ cup raisins

1 pound carrots, grated

1 orange, peeled and chopped

2 tablespoons lemon juice

2 tablespoons orange juice

1-2 teaspoons honey

½ teaspoon cinnamon

Soak the raisins in hot water for ½ hour. Drain. Combine all ingredients. Mix well. Cover. Chill for about 2 hours to blend flavors.

COLORFUL COLESLAW

Servings: 6 Preparation Time: 20-30 minutes
Chilling Time: 2 hours

Better than the common variety because of the addition of many interesting and colorful vegetables. Very low in fat, too.

2 cups green cabbage, shredded

2 cups red cabbage, shredded

½ cup carrot, diced

½ cup celery, diced

½ cup green pepper, diced

½ cup apple, chopped

½ cup cucumber, diced and peeled

¼ cup green onions, finely chopped

¼ cup parsley, chopped

3 tablespoons cider vinegar

1 tablespoon Dijon mustard

½ tablespoon low-sodium soy sauce

1 teaspoon honey

¼ teaspoon caraway seeds

¼ teaspoon celery seed

Mix the vegetables together in a large bowl. Combine the vinegar, mustard, soy sauce, and honey. Pour over the vegetables. Sprinkle caraway and celery seeds on top. Toss to mix well. Chill for about 2 hours to blend flavors.

Helpful Hints: If you have a food processor this can be prepared quite quickly.

LENTIL SALAD

Servings: 4-6 Preparation Time: 30 minutes
Cooking Time: 30 minutes Chilling Time: 3 hours

This recipe has been a real hit at many picnic potlucks. Even people who think they don't like lentils love this salad.

Salad

1 cup lentils

4 cups water

1 cup grated carrots

⅔ cup onions, finely chopped

½ cup fresh parsley, finely chopped

1 clove garlic, crushed

Dressing

1 tablespoon water

2 tablespoons red wine vinegar

2 teaspoons Dijon mustard

½ teaspoon oregano

1 teaspoon natural Worcestershire sauce (no anchovies)

1 tablespoon low-sodium soy sauce

¼ teaspoon black pepper

Cook the lentils in the water for 30 minutes, until tender but still firm. Drain. Combine with the rest of the salad ingredients. Mix the dressing ingredients together. Pour over the salad. Toss to mix. Refrigerate at least 3 hours to blend flavors.

SUPER SPROUT SALAD

Servings: 4-6 Preparation Time: 20 minutes
Cooking Time: none

What could be healthier than a sprout? The variety can be changed simply by using your favorite sprouts. Most grocery stores sell sprouted beans, but you can easily sprout your own. Just soak beans, peas and/or lentils in plain water overnight. Pour off the water, then place them on a damp paper towel until they sprout. Within 12 to 36 hours you'll have sprouts ⅛" to ½" long.

Salad

2 cups mixed sprouts (lentils, pea, aduki, etc.)

3-4 green onions, sliced

1 stalk celery, sliced

1 (2-ounce) jar chopped pimientos

¾ cup mushrooms, sliced

3-4 tablespoons fresh cilantro or parsley, chopped

Dressing

2 teaspoons Dijon mustard

1 tablespoon water

2 tablespoons white wine vinegar

1 teaspoon Worcestershire sauce

1 tablespoon low-sodium soy sauce

¼ teaspoon black pepper

Mix salad ingredients in a large bowl.

Place the mustard and the water in a small bowl and mix well. Add the remaining ingredients and mix, then pour over the sprout salad. Toss to coat.

Refrigerate before serving.

PASTA SALAD BOWL

Servings: 8 Preparation Time: 30 minutes
Cooking Time: 10 minutes Chilling Time: 2 hours

This recipe is such a universal favorite, I serve it for all the classes we presently teach.

4 cups whole wheat or vegetable pasta

1 cup broccoli or cauliflower florets

1 cup carrots, slivered

20 whole fresh snow pea pods, trimmed

½ pound fresh mushrooms, sliced

½ pint cherry tomatoes, cut in half

2 green onions, chopped

1 (2¼-ounce) can sliced black olives (optional)

1 (2-ounce) jar chopped pimiento

½ cup oil-free Italian dressing

Cook pasta in boiling water until tender, about 10 minutes. Drain. Rinse under cool water, set aside.

Steam broccoli or cauliflower, carrots and snow peas for 5 minutes.

Combine all ingredients in a large bowl. Toss to mix well. Sprinkle with some freshly ground black pepper if desired. Refrigerate at least 2 hours before serving.

Helpful Hints: Corkscrew or spiral pasta is very attractive when used in this recipe. Vegetables used can be varied to suit your family's tastes.

THREE BEAN SALAD

Servings: 8-10 Preparation Time: 30 minutes
Chilling Time: 1-2 hours

Yes, this is your old favorite bean salad—with the same great taste, but without all the fattening, health-destroying grease.

Vegetables

2 cups garbanzo beans, cooked

2 cups kidney beans, cooked

2 cups green beans, cooked

1 red onion, sliced and separated into rings

2-3 stalks celery, sliced

2 carrots, grated

1 small green pepper, cut in thin strips

4 green onions, chopped

¼ cup fresh parsley, chopped (optional)

Sauce

½ cup wine vinegar

1-2 tablespoons honey

½ teaspoon dry mustard

¼ teaspoon garlic powder

¼ teaspoon onion powder

¼ teaspoon pepper (optional)

¼ teaspoon ground cumin (optional)

Combine the vegetables in a large bowl. Combine the sauce ingredients. Pour the sauce over the vegetables and mix well. Cover and chill 1-2 hours, or more, to blend flavors.

Helpful Hint: Try ½ cup of your favorite oil-free dressing in place of the sauce.

MAIN DISHES

STUFFED PUMPKIN

Servings: 6-8 Preparation Time: 15 minutes
Cooking Time: 1½ hours

A wonderful main dish for a festive meal. I always serve this in our home for Thanksgiving and Christmas dinners. Accompany with mashed potatoes, gravy, assorted steamed vegetables and bread or a salad.

1 medium pumpkin or large winter squash	1 recipe of prepared Bread Stuffing (following)

Cut off the top of the pumpkin or squash and save it for a cover (as if you were going to make a jack-o-lantern). Clean out the seeds and stringy portion. Place the bread stuffing inside, then cover with the top of the squash. Place the pumpkin in a large roasting pan with 1 inch of water covering the bottom of pan. Bake at 350°F for 1½ hours.

BREAD STUFFING

Servings: 6-8 Preparation Time: 60 minutes
Cooking Time: 1½ hours

---

1 loaf whole wheat bread	2 teaspoons thyme
2 cups water	1 teaspoon marjoram
2 onions, chopped	2 teaspoons sage
2-3 stalks celery, chopped	½ teaspoon rosemary
1 tablespoon dried parsley	2 tablespoons low-sodium soy sauce

Cube the bread, place the cubes on a baking sheet, and toast in a 300°F oven for 15 minutes. Combine the remaining ingredients in a saucepan, bring to a boil and cook for 15 minutes. Put the toasted bread cubes into a large bowl, add the cooked liquid and toss well. Cover with a lid or plate and let rest for 15 minutes to absorb the moisture.

Bake at 350°F in a covered dish for 1½ hours, or stuff into a large winter squash or pumpkin. Bake stuffed squash for 1½ hours.

SPAGHETTI SQUASH SURPRISE

Servings: 6 Preparation Time: 20 minutes
Cooking Time: 45 minutes

The suprise is that it's squash. It's just like having pasta, but without all the calories. A large plate (2 cups) of wheat pasta has 400 calories; the same amount of spaghetti squash has only 92! And you'll love the squash.

1 spaghetti squash	4 tomatoes, chopped
1 onion, chopped	1 tablespoon lemon juice
1 clove garlic, pressed	1 tablespoon low-sodium soy sauce
1 carrot, diced	½ teaspoon basil
1 stalk celery, chopped	½ teaspoon oregano
1 green pepper, chopped	dash pepper

Cut the squash in half. Remove its seeds. Place the squash in a large pot with 2-3 inches of water. Steam for about ½ hour OR place the squash cut side down in a baking dish and bake for 45 minutes at 350°F OR microwave cut side up in a dish with a small amount of water for 10-15 minutes. Pull out cooked strands with a fork and place on platter like spaghetti. Sauté the onion, garlic, carrot, celery, and green peppers in ½ cup water for 5 minutes. Add the remaining ingredients. Cook this sauce for 10 minutes longer. Serve hot over the cooked spaghetti squash.

MU SHU TOFU

Servings: 6-8 Preparation Time: 30 minutes
Cooking Time: 20 minutes

This is the Chinese version of the burrito and is one of the most popular dishes at Chinese restaurants. Be sure to buy a quality plum sauce; its flavor will make all the difference in the taste of this dish.

½ block firm tofu (about 8-10 ounces), frozen, thawed, and cut into thin strips

1 package shiitake mushrooms

1 tablespoon fresh ginger root, grated

1 carrot, grated

1 green onion, sliced thin

6 leaves Chinese cabbage, sliced thin

1 cup bean sprouts

another vegetable, julienne sliced (optional)

½ teaspoon Chinese five-spice mixture

¼ cup low-sodium soy sauce

1 tablespoon sherry (optional)

2 tablespoons cornstarch

Chinese plum sauce

whole wheat chapatis

Pour 2 cups boiling water over the mushrooms and allow them to soak while slicing the other vegetables. Drain the mushrooms, cut off their hard stems and discard. Slice the mushroom caps into thin strips.

In ¼ cup water, sauté the ginger, carrot, and any optional long-cooking vegetable for 5 minutes. Add the onions, cabbage, bean sprouts, mushrooms, and any optional fast-cooking vegetable. Add the five-spice, soy sauce, sherry and 1 tablespoon plum sauce. Cook and stir for 5 minutes more. Add the tofu strips. Add the cornstarch dissolved in ⅓ cup cold water. Bring to a boil and stir until the sauce thickens.

To serve, spread about ½ teaspoon of plum sauce down the center of a warm chapati. Add some of the vegetable-tofu mixture and roll up the chapati.

Helpful Hints: Try this vegetable-tofu mixture served over rice or other whole grains.

VEGETABLE CHOP SUEY

Servings: 6-8 Preparation Time: 45 minutes
Cooking Time: 30 minutes

Everything you like about chop suey, but without the unappetizing grease. This recipe makes the conventional dish you'll find in any Chinese restaurant. If you prefer more distinctive or unusual flavors, add exotic spices like lemon grass.

¼ cup water	1 cup snow peas (optional)
2 cloves garlic, crushed	½ cup green onions, sliced in 1-inch pieces
2 onions, sliced	1 cup mung bean sprouts
8-10 leaves Chinese cabbage, sliced	3 tablespoons low-sodium soy sauce
1 stalk celery, sliced	2 tablespoons sherry (optional)
¼ pound broccoli, sliced	3 cups water
¼ pound mushrooms, sliced	5-6 tablespoons arrowroot or cornstarch

Put ¼ cup water into a large pot or wok. Add the crushed garlic and heat the water to boiling. Add the onions, celery, cabbage, and broccoli. Sauté about 10 minutes. Add the mushrooms. Sauté 5 more minutes. Add the water, soy sauce, sherry, green onions, snow peas, and bean sprouts. Bring to a boil and cook about 10 minutes. Dissolve the arrowroot or cornstarch in a small amount of cold water. Remove the pot from the heat. Gradually add the arrowroot or cornstarch mixture, stirring well. Return to the heat. Stir until thickened. Serve over brown rice, whole wheat spaghetti or buckwheat soba noodles.

Helpful Hints: Prepare the rice before starting to cook the vegetables. Keep the rice warm until serving. If you prefer noodles, have the water boiling while the vegetables are cooking. About 15 minutes before serving, drop the noodles into the boiling water, return to a boil, reduce the heat, and simmer about 10 minutes.

HEATHER'S MUSHROOM DELIGHT

Yield: about 4 cups   Preparation Time: 20 minutes
Cooking Time: 15 minutes

This dish is named for our daughter because it was her favorite dish when she was 5 years old. When we taught cooking classes in Hawaii, the participants always prepared this dish. It's that simple, that easy, and always a success. Dried mushrooms give it a chewy "meaty" texture.

3 packages dried mushrooms (shiitake)

1 round onion, chopped

1 bunch green onions, chopped

2 cloves garlic, crushed

1½ tablespoons fresh ginger root

¼ cup sherry (or apple juice)

⅓ cup low-sodium soy sauce

1 cup mushroom stock

2 cups water

⅓ cup cornstarch or arrowroot

Place the mushrooms in a bowl. Pour 2 cups of boiling water over them. Soak for 15 minutes. Squeeze to remove the excess water. Cut off their tough stems and discard. Chop the mushroom caps into bite-sized pieces. Set aside. Strain and reserve 1 cup mushroom stock.

Place the chopped round onion in a saucepan with ¼ cup water. Sauté for 5 minutes. Add the chopped green onion and chopped mushrooms, garlic, ginger, sherry, and soy sauce. Mix well. Add the mushroom stock and water. Heat to boiling, stirring frequently.

In a separate bowl, mix the cornstarch or arrowroot in ½ cup water. Add to the sauce. Continue to cook and stir until thickened. Serve over whole grains.

SHISH-KEBABS

Servings: 6-8 Preparation Time: 60 minutes
Cooking Time: 15 minutes

These kebabs lend themselves nicely to a barbecue on the outdoor grill. If you're having mixed company for dinner, it's a simple matter of adding the meat they think they're missing to a skewer. You also won't stick out if you take these to a barbecue.

Marinade

¾ cup vinegar

1¼ cups tomato juice

¼ cup red wine (or apple juice)

¼ cup low-sodium soy sauce

¼ teaspoon garlic powder

1 teaspoon basil

1 teaspoon oregano

Vegetables

1 pound mushrooms

4 long eggplants

2 green peppers

1 pound boiling onions

6 tomatoes

In a large bowl, mix together the ingredients for the marinade. Set aside. Cut the eggplant into 1-inch slices, place them on a dry baking sheet, and broil them 8 inches from broiler about 5 minutes until browned (watch them; they can burn easily). Add eggplant to the marinade. Clean the mushrooms, but leave them whole unless they are very large. Add the mushrooms to the marinade. Stir well to make sure the mushrooms and eggplant are well coated with marinade. Let them stand at room temperature at least 3 hours.

Clean the onions and cut them in half. Cut the peppers into 1-inch chunks. Cut the tomatoes into wedges. Skewer the vegetables in any order you choose. I find that long bamboo skewers work best. Place the skewers on a broiling tray (or on a rack in a baking dish). Broil at least 8 inches from heat for 10-15 minutes. Watch them carefully. You may baste them with extra marinade as they broil, if desired. Serve at once.

Helpful Hints: Serve with brown rice or bulgur wheat. A good dish for guests or a special occasion. A delicious sauce for this meal can be made by adding 3 tablespoons of arrowroot or cornstarch to the marinade, placing the mixture in a saucepan over medium heat, cooking, and stirring until thickened.

EGGPLANT CREOLE

Servings: 8 Preparation Time: 30 minutes
Cooking Time: 30 minutes

A fast and easy eggplant recipe and a favorite with everyone except John, who hates eggplant.

2 eggplants, cut into chunks

2 onions, chopped

2 green peppers, chopped

2 cloves garlic, pressed

3 cups canned tomatoes

1 tablespoon low-sodium soy sauce

½ teaspoon basil

½ teaspoon thyme

1 cup whole wheat breadcrumbs

Sauté the onion, garlic, green pepper, and eggplant in ½ cup water for 5 minutes. Add the tomatoes, breaking them up with a fork. Stir in the seasonings. Cook until the eggplant is tender, about 20 minutes. Place this mixture in a large baking dish. Sprinkle with the bread crumbs. Bake at 350°F for 30 minutes.

BRAZILIAN BLACK BEANS WITH MARINATED TOMATOES

Servings: 6-8 Preparation Time: 30 minutes
Cooking Time: 3 hours (beans)

This is John's favorite black bean dish. We serve it at the McDougall Program at St. Helena Hospital where it is prepared without the vinegar because of Seventh Day Adventist beliefs. Vinegar is available on the dinner tables in bottles, and when I remember to tell the patients to try it, this dish goes up many points in ratings.

Beans

2 cups dried black beans

6 cups water

2 large garlic cloves

1 onion, studded with 8 cloves

2 onions, chopped

1 large green pepper, chopped

Place beans and water in a large pot. Add the 2 whole garlic cloves and 1 whole onion, studded with 8 whole cloves. (Make a small hole for each clove in the side of the onion with a toothpick; then push the stem end into the hole.) Cook over low heat about 2 hours. Remove the garlic and the whole onion. Add the chopped onions and green pepper. Cook an additional hour until the beans are tender.

Marinated Tomatoes
Chilling Time: 1 hour

6 tomatoes, chopped

1 bunch green onions, chopped

½ onion, chopped

1 clove garlic, crushed

3 tablespoons wine vinegar

4-5 dashes Tabasco™ sauce

Combine all the ingredients. Refrigerate until ready to serve, at least 1 hour. Serve the beans over brown rice with some of the marinated tomatoes on top.

POTATO PANCAKES

Servings: 6 Preparation Time: 30 minutes
Cooking Time: 15 minutes

An American favorite—it would be downright un-American not to like these. Serve with applesauce, ketchup, or gravy. If you have a nonstick griddle or frying pan, you will not need to oil it before using.

½ raw onion, grated

2 large potatoes, grated (if organic, don't peel, just scrub well)

4 tablespoons whole wheat flour

4 tablespoons water

2 tablespoons parsley, chopped

Mix all the ingredients in a bowl. Lightly oil a griddle and heat to 325°F or medium heat. Ladle the potato mixture onto the griddle, flattening it slightly. Cook about 8-10 minutes on the first side; turn and cook an additional 5-8 minutes.

TAMALE PIE

Servings: 8 Preparation Time: 45 minutes
Cooking Time: 45 minutes

We serve this to our patients in the McDougall Program at St. Helena, and it's my favorite use of cornmeal. A great dish for preparing ahead of time, Tamale Pie can be kept in the refrigerator and baked later, so you can do other things around dinner time—like visiting with family and friends instead of cooking.

3 cups cooked pinto beans, mashed	1 green pepper, chopped
1 onion, chopped	1-2 green chilis, chopped
1½ teaspoons chili powder	1½ cups cornmeal
¼ cup tomato sauce	2½ cups water
1 cup frozen corn	½ teaspoon chili powder

Place the onion in a large pot with ¼ cup water. Sauté about 10 minutes, add the green pepper, corn, green chilis, tomato sauce, and chili powder. Cook 5 minutes. Add the mashed beans and cook about 10 minutes over low heat. Remove from the heat.

Combine the cornmeal, water, and chili powder in a saucepan. Cook over medium heat until the mixture thickens. Stir constantly with a wire whisk or the cornmeal will lump.

Using a nonstick 8" × 8" pan, spread half of the cornmeal mixture over the bottom. Pour the bean mixture over this and spread it out. Then use a spatula to evenly spread the remaining cornmeal mixture over the top.

Bake at 350°F for 45 minutes or until it bubbles.

STUFFED PEPPERS

Servings: 8 Preparation Time: 45 minutes
Cooking Time: 1¼ hours

Another recipe we serve for our McDougall Program patients at St. Helena Hospital. Everyone enjoys the flavorful filling. These stuffed peppers can be prepared ahead of time. Keep them in the refrigerator until ready to bake, and add 15 minutes to the required baking time. As a variation, use 1 cup of corn, fresh or frozen, in place of 1 cup of rice. The green peppers can also be steamed before stuffing, if desired. Place stemmed and cored peppers in a steaming basket. Steam over 1 inch of boiling water for 5 minutes. Stuff and bake as below.

8 large green peppers, stemmed and cored	3 cups brown rice, cooked
1 onion, diced	1 teaspoon thyme
½ cup celery, chopped	1 teaspoon sage
½ pound mushrooms, chopped	½ teaspoon basil
¼ cup water	¼ teaspoon garlic powder
2 cups tomato sauce (1 cup for topping)	

Cook the onions, celery, and mushrooms in the water for about 15 minutes, until tender. Mix in 1 cup tomato sauce, rice, and seasonings. Pack the mixture into raw green peppers that have been stemmed and cored. Place in a 9" × 12" baking dish.

Pour the remaining 1 cup tomato sauce over the peppers, a little on each. Add about 1½ cups water to the bottom of the baking dish to prevent peppers from drying out. Cover and bake at 375°F for 45 minutes, uncover and bake for 15 minutes longer.

GARBANZO STEW

Servings: 8-10 Preparation Time: 15 minutes
Cooking Time: 3 hours

Now served in the McDougall Program at St. Helena Hospital, this stew was originally created by the staff of the Castle Hospital food service and served in the employee cafeteria back in the late '70s in Kailua, Hawaii.

2 cups dry garbanzo beans (chick peas)

10 cups water

2 potatoes, cut in chunks

2 tablespoons low-sodium soy sauce (optional)

2 carrots, thickly sliced

2 stalks celery, thickly sliced

2 onions, chopped

Place the garbanzos and water in a large pot. Bring to a boil, reduce the heat to medium low, cover and cook at least 2 hours. Add the remaining ingredients and cook until tender, usually 1 hour more, depending on how soft you like your vegetables.

Helpful Hints: This may also be made in a slow cooker. Add all the ingredients at once and cook on high temperature for 8 hours or more.

QUICK CONFETTI RICE

Servings: 6   Preparation Time: 15 minutes
Cooking Time: 15 minutes

Nathan and Ilene Pritikin enjoyed this dish so much, they asked if they could use it in their book, *The Pritikin Promise* (Simon and Shuster, 1983).

1 onion, chopped	½ teaspoon oregano
1 green pepper, chopped	½ teaspoon paprika
1 cup broccoli, chopped	4 cups rice, cooked
2 cups corn kernels	1 tablespoon low-sodium soy sauce
2 tomatoes, chopped	

Sauté the vegetables, except the tomatoes, in ½ cup water for 10 minutes. Add the seasonings, tomatoes, and rice. Stir until heated through, about 5 minutes.

Helpful Hints: Use frozen vegetables to save on preparation time. Try varying the vegetables using whatever is in season. Make sure the pieces are small so that all cook in the same amount of time.

PEASANT'S PIE

Servings: 6-8 Preparation Time: 1 hour
Cooking Time: 30-45 minutes

A satisfying Shepherd's Pie without the meat, this dish can be made in a jiffy if you have leftover mashed potatoes.

Topping

4 medium potatoes, cooked and mashed

(mash with about ¼ cup water, not with milk or butter) to yield 3 cups mashed

Sauce

2 cups brown gravy, mushroom gravy, or other sauces (try tomato)

Filling

1 onion, coarsely chopped

3 carrots, sliced thinly

1 green pepper, diced

½ pound broccoli, cut into stems and florets

¼ pound green beans, cut into 1-inch pieces

1 bunch spinach, torn into bite-sized pieces

Steam the vegetables (except the spinach) about 15 minutes until crisp-tender. Remove from the heat. Stir in the spinach and 2 cups gravy. Spoon this filling into a 9" × 12" baking dish. Spread the mashed potatoes over the top. Sprinkle with a small amount of paprika. Bake 30 minutes at 350°F.

Helpful Hints: Add ½ pound Brussels sprouts if they are available. Use your favorite vegetables, cut into bite-sized pieces, for filling. Use about 8 cups of chopped vegetables. If this casserole is prepared ahead and refrigerated, add 15 minutes to the baking time. Use leftover vegetables, adding to the others after they have been steamed. Frozen vegetables can also be used. Peas and corn are especially good additions.

LIMA BEAN JAMBALAYA

Servings: 8 Preparation Time: 30 minutes
Cooking Time: 3 hours

This recipe not only makes a delicious soup, but a wonderful topping for whole grains or delicious filling for pita bread or tortillas. This dish was always a big hit at our monthly potlucks in Hawaii. We had to have these potluck dinners in order to keep in touch with our patients since, unlike a traditional medical practice, our patients got well and had no need to come back to their doctor.

7 cups water	1 tomato, chopped
2½ cups dry lima beans	½ cup frozen corn
2½ cups pumpkin, cut up	½ cup frozen lima beans
1 large onion, chopped	1 teaspoon savory
2 stalks celery, chopped	1 tablespoon low-sodium soy sauce
1 clove garlic, crushed	

Place lima beans in water in large pot. Bring to a boil, cover, and simmer for 2 hours. Add the pumpkin, onion, celery, garlic, and seasonings. Cook for 30 minutes, then add the remaining ingredients and cook for 30 minutes longer.

AUTUMN BARLEY STEW

Servings: 8-10 Preparation Time: 20 minutes
Cooking Time: 60 minutes

I invented this because I like Brussels sprouts and couldn't find any recipes featuring this favorite vegetable.

1½ cups barley

10 cups water

2 onions, chopped in large pieces

3 white potatoes, cut in chunks

1 large yam, cut in chunks

1 pound Brussels sprouts

2 tablespoons low-sodium soy sauce

1 tablespoon parsley flakes

2 teaspoons oregano

1 teaspoon dill weed

3 tomatoes, cut in wedges

Place the barley and water in a large pot. Bring to a boil. Add the remaining ingredients, except the tomatoes. Reduce the heat, cover, and simmer about 50 minutes. Add the tomatoes. Cook an additional 10 minutes. Serve hot.

Helpful Hints: If you make this stew in a slow cooker, do not add the tomatoes until just before serving.

POLYNESIAN VEGETABLES

Servings: 4-6 Preparation Time: 15-20 minutes
Cooking Time: 20 minutes

In our early days in Hawaii, we all but lived on sweet and sour meat dishes (pork, chicken, fish, etc.). When we eliminated fat-laden foods from our diet, we didn't want to give up this highly flavorful dish, so with a few creative modifications, I created Polynesian Vegetables.

1 onion, chopped

½ cup water

1 (8-ounce) can pineapple chunks (unsweet-ened)

1 green pepper, cut in 1 inch pieces

2 cups assorted vegetables, chopped

1½ teaspoons fresh ginger root, grated

2 tablespoons low-sodium soy sauce

1 tablespoon cornstarch or arrowroot

1 (8-ounce) can water chestnuts, drained

In a large saucepan, sauté the onion in ¼ cup water about 5 minutes. Drain the pineapple, reserving the juice. Set aside the pineapple chunks and ¼ cup of the juice. Pour the remainder of the juice into the saucepan; add the green pepper, vegetables, water, ginger, and soy sauce. Bring to a boil. Reduce the heat, cover, and simmer about 10 minutes. Mix the cornstarch with the ¼ cup of pineapple juice and add to the saucepan. Cook and stir until the mixture boils and thickens. Add the water chestnuts and pineapple chunks. Heat through. Serve over rice or other whole grains.

Helpful Hints: Many vegetables are delicious in this dish. Use your own favorites or try one or two of the following: broccoli cuts, halved Brussels sprouts, sliced carrots, cauliflower pieces, green beans, pea pods, or sliced zucchini.

QUICK VEGETABLE STEW

Servings: 6 Preparation Time: 10 minutes
Cooking Time: 20-30 minutes

Quick, easy, healthful, and delicious as is—or turn this dish into a curry stew by omitting the marjoram, thyme and wine, and using 3 teaspoons of curry powder instead.

2 onions, sliced	2 cloves garlic, crushed
3 cups water	½ teaspoon marjoram
¼ cup low-sodium soy sauce	½ teaspoon thyme
¼ cup red wine (optional)	8 cups assorted chopped frozen vegetables
1 teaspoon fresh ginger, grated	3 tablespoons cornstarch or arrowroot

In a large pan, sauté the onions, garlic and ginger in ½ cup water for 5 minutes. Add the marjoram and thyme. Mix well. Add the remaining water, soy sauce (and wine, if desired). Bring to a boil. Add the vegetables, stir. When the mixture boils again, reduce the heat to medium-low, cover, and cook until tender, usually 15-20 minutes, depending on the size of the vegetables. Mix cornstarch or arrowroot in ¼ cup cold water. Slowly add to the cooked stew, stirring constantly until it thickens. Serve over rice or other grains.

MEDITERRANEAN MUSHROOMS

Servings: 6-8 Preparation Time: 25 minutes
Cooking Time: 25 minutes

Save the stems of the mushrooms and chop for your next batch of spaghetti sauce. Freeze until ready to use. Save some preparation time by preparing the mushrooms while the other vegetables are cooking. This dish is also very good cold as an appetizer.

1 large onion, sliced	1 tablespoon parsley flakes
1 leek, sliced	1 tablespoon thyme leaves
2 carrots, sliced	1 bay leaf
2 celery stalks, sliced	freshly ground pepper (optional)
2 cloves garlic, crushed	2 pounds mushrooms
3 tomatoes, cut into wedges	2 tablespoons arrowroot or cornstarch
1 cup white wine (or apple juice)	

Prepare mushrooms by cleaning and removing their stems. Leave whole if they are small, otherwise cut in half. Set aside.

In a large pot, sauté the onion, leek, carrots, celery, and garlic in ½ cup water for 10 minutes. Stir in the wine, tomatoes, and seasonings. Bring to a boil, lower the heat, and add the prepared mushrooms. Simmer over medium-low heat for 10 minutes, stirring occasionally.

Mix the arrowroot or cornstarch with ¼ cup water. Slowly add to the mushroom mixture while stirring. Cook and stir until thickened. Serve over rice, other whole grains, or pasta.

WICKED MUSHROOMS

Servings: 4 Preparation Time: 15 minutes
Cooking Time: 60 minutes

Served at the McDougall Program at St. Helena Hospital, but without the wine because it is a Seventh Day Adventist Hospital. I think wine provides a more distinctive taste than grape juice, but try both and see which you prefer.

1½ pounds mushrooms, cut in quarters

1 onion, chopped

1 green pepper, cut in medium chunks

2 cups water

2 bay leaves

¼ teaspoon thyme

1 tablespoon low-sodium soy sauce

1 cup burgundy wine (or grape juice)

¼ cup tomato paste

1 tablespoon parsley flakes

freshly ground pepper

Put ½ cup water in a large cooking pot. Add the chopped onion, bay leaves, and thyme. Sauté about 5 minutes. Add the chopped green pepper and mushrooms. Continue cooking for about 10 minutes.

Add the remaining water, soy sauce, wine, tomato paste, and parsley. Add a little fresh-ground pepper, if desired. Simmer slowly over low heat for at least 60 minutes, until the liquid becomes a thick sauce. Remove bay leaves. Serve very hot over brown rice.

SPAGHETTI SAUCE

Servings: 4   Preparation Time: 30 minutes
Cooking Time: 2 hours

A very traditional Italian red sauce. The spices you use will make all the difference in terms of its appeal to your family, so change any spices you wish to make this sauce more "like Mom used to make." For an extra special sauce, add a handful of dried tomatoes plus an extra cup of water for them to soak up.

4 tablespoons water	1½ teaspoons oregano
1 onion, chopped	2 cups tomato sauce
½ green pepper, chopped	6 fresh tomatoes, chopped
3 celery stalks, chopped	2 bay leaves
½ pound mushrooms, sliced	1 teaspoon basil
2 garlic cloves, pressed	

Sauté the onion, green pepper, celery, mushrooms, and garlic in the water for 10 minutes. Add the remaining ingredients. Simmer, uncovered, for about 2 hours. Serve over spaghetti. (Try whole wheat, vegetable, or spinach spaghetti—all are delicious.) Cook whole wheat spaghetti and spinach spaghetti 5-10 minutes. Whole wheat pasta has much more fiber than the vegetable varieties.

Helpful Hints: If you like eggplant, add some diced eggplant and sauté with the other vegetables. One large can of tomatoes (28 ounces) can be substituted for the fresh tomatoes. Try serving this sauce over spaghetti squash. To cook spaghetti squash: Cut the squash in half. Remove its seeds. Place it in large pot with 2-3 inches of water. Steam for about ½ hour. Pull out cooked strands with a fork.

WHITE MUSHROOM SAUCE

Servings: 6 Preparation Time: 15 minutes
Cooking Time: 30 minutes

This sauce is delicious over spaghetti noodles or whole grains. Using dried mushrooms gives this dish a chewy "meaty" texture. Using a nut milk will make it richer, but also higher in fat.

3 cups nut milk or rice milk

1 cup water

1 onion, chopped

2 packages dried mushrooms, sliced, OR 1 pound fresh mushrooms, sliced

½ teaspoon tarragon

¼ teaspoon dill weed

¼ teaspoon thyme

¼ cup sherry

3 tablespoons cornstarch or arrowroot

Soak the dried mushrooms in warm water for 15 minutes. Squeeze out excess water and slice. Sauté onion in ¼ cup water for 5 minutes. Add the remaining ingredients, except for the cornstarch or arrowroot. Bring to a boil over low heat, stirring often. Mix the cornstarch or arrowroot in ⅓ cup water. Add to the white sauce. Continue to cook and stir until thickened.

SPANISH RICE

Servings: 4-6 Preparation Time: 20 minutes
Cooking Time: 30 minutes

A traditional recipe familiar to most people, but greatly improved by leaving out the fattening grease. We serve this at the McDougall Program at St. Helena Hospital.

3 cups cooked brown rice

1 onion, chopped

1 green pepper, chopped

1 stalk celery, chopped (optional)

½ cup mushrooms, chopped

1 green chili pepper, chopped

2 cloves garlic, crushed

1 cup tomato sauce

1 tablespoon low-sodium soy sauce

Sauté the onion, green pepper, celery, mushrooms, and garlic in ½ cup water for about 15 minutes. Use a large pot. Add the tomato sauce, soy sauce, and the green chili pepper. Mix well. Add the cooked rice. Heat about 15 minutes. Serve hot.

Helpful Hints: Use 2 green chili peppers if you like spicy foods. Try adding ½ teaspoon basil and ½ teaspoon oregano.

TOSSED GREEN RICE

Servings: 4 Preparation Time: 10 minutes
Cooking Time: 1 hour

This is like a hot rice salad. John's favorite rice dish, it can be a simple complete meal or a side dish for a more elaborate dinner. It leaves you satisfied, but never uncomfortably stuffed.

4 cups hot, cooked brown rice

2 tablespoons water

1½ cups green onions (2 bunches), chopped

2 stalks celery, sliced

1 green pepper, chopped

1 clove garlic, crushed

½ cup parsley, finely chopped

½ teaspoon basil

¼ teaspoon paprika

½ teaspoon dill weed

2 tomatoes, chopped

Begin cooking the rice about 45 minutes before you start to cook the vegetables. The rice should be hot. Sauté the green onions, celery, green pepper, and garlic in 2 tablespoons water for 5 minutes. Add the parsley, basil, dill, and paprika. Cook about 5 minutes longer.

Put the hot brown rice in a large serving bowl. Add the sautéed vegetables. Toss to mix well. Then add the chopped tomatoes. Toss lightly and serve at once.

"Fried" Rice

Servings: 4 Preparation Time: 15 minutes
Cooking Time: 20 minutes

This was John's first rice dish. He learned it from an old girlfriend who was from Hawaii. However, if he'd married her, he would have died of a heart attack from all the pork fat she cooked the rice in. I modified the recipe, saved his life—and made his tastebuds happy too!

3 cups mixed vegetables, chopped	¼ cup water
Examples:	2 cups cooked brown rice
carrots, onions, broccoli: 1 cup each	1 tablespoon low-sodium soy sauce
green pepper, carrots, bean sprouts: 1 cup each	½ teaspoon dry mustard
carrots, bean sprouts, green onions: 1 cup each	½ teaspoon ground ginger

Mix the mustard and ginger with ¼ cup water in a large soup pot. Heat to boiling. Add the vegetables and cook over medium heat until tender (about 10-15 minutes). Use a wok if you have one. If the vegetables are cut in small strips they will cook faster. Add the cooked rice; stir until heated. Add the soy sauce. Mix well. Continue cooking until heated through (1-2 minutes).

Helpful Hints: This will serve two hungry people for a fast, complete meal. Any combination of vegetables may be used. Just keep the pieces small so they cook quickly.

STUFFED CABBAGE ROLLS

Servings: 6-8 (14 rolls) Preparation Time: 45 minutes
Cooking Time: 45 minutes

A great all-American dish. The healthy modifications in this recipe will leave you saying, "All I gave up was bad health and obesity when I switched to McDougall-style eating."

1 head cabbage	⅛ teaspoon garlic powder
1 onion, chopped	dash pepper (optional)
½ pound mushrooms, chopped	3 cups cooked brown rice
¼ cup currants (optional)	4 cups tomato sauce
¼ teaspoon nutmeg	

Remove the core from the cabbage. Steam over boiling water for 5 minutes. Let cool slightly. Peel off the leaves carefully and set aside. Sauté the onions, mushrooms, and currants in ½ cup water for 10 minutes. Stir in nutmeg, garlic powder, and pepper. Stir in the brown rice and 1 cup of the tomato sauce. Remove from the heat. Pour 1 cup of the tomato sauce over the bottom of a 9" × 12" baking dish. Spoon about ⅓ to ½ cup rice mixture into the center of each cabbage leaf. Roll up and place seam side down in baking dish. Pour the remaining tomato sauce over the rolls in the baking dish. Cover and bake at 350°F for 45 minutes.

Helpful Hints: The cabbage rolls can be prepared in advance. They keep well in the refrigerator for up to a full day before baking. If refrigerated, bake just before serving and add 15 minutes to required baking time.

VEGETABLE STUFFED PEPPERS WITH SPICY TOMATO SAUCE

Servings: 6 Preparation Time: 40 minutes
Cooking Time: 45 minutes

The extra work of cutting up more interesting vegetables for this recipe will be appreciated. The spicing is unique. You'll never be accused of making bland meals when you serve this.

Stuffing

6 large green peppers

½ cup water

1 onion, chopped

1 clove garlic, crushed

1 teaspoon ginger root, minced

1 tomato, chopped

2 stalks celery, chopped

3 green onions, sliced

2 cups fresh or frozen corn kernels

2½ cups cooked brown rice

1 tablespoon low-sodium soy sauce

½ teaspoon chili powder blend

Sauce

2 cups tomato sauce

1 small onion, quartered

½ green pepper (use 3-4 tops of peppers)

2-3 drops Tabasco™ sauce

¼ teaspoon basil

¼ teaspoon oregano

1 tablespoon parsley flakes

Begin by preparing the peppers. Cut off their tops (reserve for later use), clean out the insides, and steam them over 1 inch of boiling water for 5 minutes (steaming is an optional step). In a large pan, sauté the onion, garlic, and ginger for 5 minutes. Add the tomato, celery, green onions, and corn. Cook for 5 minutes longer. Add the rice and seasonings. Stir to mix well. Remove from the heat. Pack the mixture into the green pepper shells. Combine all the ingredients for the tomato sauce in a blender. Blend until smooth. Pour over the peppers in a 9" × 12" baking dish. Cover, bake at 350°F for 30 minutes, uncover, and bake an additional 15 minutes.

Helpful Hints: May be prepared ahead and baked just before eating.

EASY RATATOUILLE

Servings: 8-10 Preparation Time: 20 minutes
Cooking Time: 60 minutes

A traditional French dish. Make this extra special by using fresh herbs instead of dried ones in twice the amounts given below.

2 large onions, chopped

2 green peppers, cut in chunks

6 zucchini, sliced

2 large eggplant, cut in chunks

2 cloves garlic, crushed

4 cups chopped tomatoes (fresh or canned with their juice)

1 tablespoon basil

1 tablespoon oregano

2 tablespoons parsley flakes

Place all the ingredients in a large pot. Cover. Cook over medium-low heat about 60 minutes. Stir occasionally. Serve hot or cold.

Helpful Hints: Serve over noodles, grains, potatoes, or stuffed in pita bread. This recipe makes a large amount but freezes and reheats well. It can be made in a slow cooker. Just add all the ingredients at once and cook on low about 6-8 hours.

STOVE TOP STEW

Servings: 8 Preparation Time: 45 minutes
Cooking Time: 60 minutes

Make this stew ahead and reheat just before serving. Try using other vegetables instead of the optional ones suggested.

3 onions, sliced

4 cloves garlic, pressed

4 potatoes, cut in chunks

4 stalks celery, sliced

4 carrots, sliced

2 zucchini, cut in chunks (optional)

½ pound mushrooms, sliced (optional)

1 stalk broccoli, sliced (optional)

1 (28-ounce) can tomatoes chopped

2 tablespoons molasses

1 tablespoon parsley flakes

2 teaspoons dill weed

¾ cup burgundy wine (or apple juice)

3 tablespoons arrowroot or cornstarch

Put ½ cup water in a large pot, and add the onions, garlic, potatoes, celery, and carrots. Sauté about 15 minutes. Add broccoli if desired, along with the burgundy wine. Cover and steam the vegetables about 10 minutes. Add the tomatoes, molasses, parsley, and dill. Add zucchini and mushrooms if desired. Cover and simmer over low heat about 30 minutes longer. Mix arrowroot or cornstarch in ⅓ cup water. Gradually add to stew, stirring constantly until thickened.

BAKED EGGPLANT CASSEROLE

Servings: 6-8 Preparation Time: 30 minutes
Cooking Time: 10 minutes (prebake); 45 minutes (casserole)

One of my and my daughter's favorite recipes, this Baked Eggplant Casserole is now served at the deli bar at our exercise club.

2 medium or 3 small round eggplants	1 (2-ounce) jar pimiento, chopped
½ cup cornmeal	4 cups tomato sauce
¼ teaspoon garlic powder	1 teaspoon basil
1 large onion, sliced in rings	½ teaspoon oregano
1 large green pepper, sliced in rings	

Cut eggplant into ½-inch thick slices. Mix cornmeal and garlic powder, and dip the eggplant slices in this mixture until both sides are well coated. Place the eggplant slices on a dry baking sheet. Bake at 400°F for 10 minutes.

Meanwhile prepare onion, pepper, and pimiento. Combine the tomato sauce, basil, and oregano.

Arrange baked eggplant slices in the bottom of a 9" × 12" baking dish. Lay the onion and pepper rings on top of the eggplant; scatter the chopped pimiento over all of this.

Pour the tomato sauce mixture over the vegetables. Bake, uncovered, in a 375°F oven for 45 minutes.

Helpful Hints: You can use a smaller casserole dish. Just arrange the casserole in two layers: eggplant, onions, peppers, and sauce; then repeat.

BUDDHA'S DELIGHT

Servings: 8 Preparation Time: 30 minutes
Cooking Time: 25-30 minutes

Buddha's delight is a popular vegetarian dish in China. There are many variations, but one thing they share is that at least 10 different vegetables are used in the preparation.

Vegetables

4 cups broccoli florets (or use some cauliflower with the broccoli)

2 cups bok choy, sliced thinly

2 cups mushrooms, sliced

2 cups snow peas

1½ cups carrots, sliced

½ cup green onions, sliced

½ cup water chestnuts, sliced

½ cup bamboo shoots, sliced

½ cup whole straw mushrooms (canned)

1 cup whole baby corn (canned)

Sauce

1½ cups water

2 tablespoons sherry (or apple juice)

4 tablespoons low-sodium soy sauce

3 tablespoons cornstarch or arrowroot

¼ teaspoon white pepper

Prepare the vegetables as directed and set aside. Combine the sauce ingredients in a separate bowl and set aside.

In a wok or a large saucepan, place about ½ cup water and a dash or two of soy sauce. Heat until it boils, then add the broccoli, carrots, and green onions. Cook and stir for about 10 minutes.

Add the mushrooms, bok choy and snow peas. Cook and stir for 5 minutes.

Add the bamboo shoots and water chestnuts. Cook and stir a few more minutes.

Add the sauce mixture to the pan. Bring to a boil, stirring constantly. After mixture boils and thickens, stir in the straw mushrooms and baby corn. Cook until heated thoroughly. Serve over brown rice.

HEARTY POTATO VEGETABLE CURRY

Servings: 6 Preparation Time: 30 minutes
Cooking Time: 1¼ hours

A wonderful curry dish with the exotic added flavors of apple and chutney.

2½ cups water

1 (16-ounce) can tomatoes, chopped, with juice

3 white potatoes, chopped

1 onion, cut in wedges

2 cloves garlic, crushed

½ pound mushrooms, cut in half

1 red or green pepper, chopped

1 green apple, peeled and diced

1 tablespoon curry powder

1 teaspoon ground coriander

½ teaspoon ground cumin

2 tablespoons whole wheat flour

¼ cup water

3 tablespoons chutney

1 zucchini, coarsely chopped

1½ cups frozen peas

Place the water, tomatoes, and the tomato juice in a large pot. Add the potatoes, onion, garlic, mushrooms, pepper, apple, and spices. Bring to a boil, then reduce heat to simmer.

Mix the flour and water. Add to the vegetable mixture. Mix in well. Cover and simmer for 30 minutes

Stir in the chutney, peas, and zucchini. Cook uncovered 30 minutes longer. Serve over brown rice.

SUMMER VEGETABLE DELIGHT

Servings: 3-4 Preparation Time: 20 minutes
Cooking Time: 20 minutes

This may be made using a variety of other vegetables. Substitute your favorites in equivalent amounts for a fast, easy meal. Choose favorite seasonings from the list or use your own imagination.

1 onion, sliced	1 cup green bean pieces
8 medium mushrooms, sliced	2 tomatoes, chopped
1 green pepper, cut in ½ inch pieces	1 cup corn kernels
1 to 2 zucchini, sliced	2 tablespoons low-sodium soy sauce

Suggested Seasonings

½ teaspoon basil	1 teaspoon cumin
½ teaspoon oregano	or
1 tablespoon parsley	½ teaspoon basil
or	½ teaspoon dill weed
1 tablespoon chopped fresh cilantro	½ teaspoon cumin
½ teaspoon turmeric	½ teaspoon paprika

Sauté the onions and mushrooms in ½ cup water for 5 minutes. Add the remaining vegetables and seasonings, plus ½ cup water. Cover and simmer over medium low heat for 15 minutes. Stir occasionally. Mix 1 tablespoon cornstarch or arrowroot in ¼ cup cold water. Add to the vegetable mixture while stirring. Cook and stir until thickened. Serve over rice, potatoes, or whole wheat bread.

CAJUN BEAN STEW

Servings: 8 Preparation Time: 30 minutes
Cooking Time: 2½ hours

A delicious way to eat your dark green leafy vegetables. You can make it mild or spicy by changing the amount of Louisana Hot Sauce™ you add.

1 pound dried black-eyed peas	1 sweet potato, sliced
1 cup dried lima beans	Several dashes of Louisiana Hot Sauce™
8 cups water	1½ teaspoons Cajun Spices (see page 117)
2 cups corn (frozen)	4 cups greens (kale, mustard greens, spinach, swiss chard), shredded
2 cups okra (frozen)	

Place the black-eyed peas and lima beans in a large pot with 8 cups of water. Bring to a boil, reduce the heat, cover and cook for 1½ hours. Add the corn, okra (cut in pieces if desired), sweet potato, onion, and seasonings. Cover and cook an additional 30 minutes. Add the greens and cook about 30 minutes.

Helpful Hints: Pass the Louisiana Hot Sauce™ at the table to shake on individual servings, if desired.

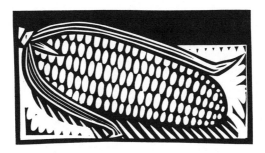

SPICY LENTIL FILLING

Servings: 8-10 Preparation Time: 15 minutes
Cooking Time: 1½ hours

This filling also makes a wonderful sandwich spread when cold. It will keep several days in the refrigerator and also freezes well. This is a meal that could easily be prepared over the weekend, refrigerated and then heated up for a fast meal during the week.

2 onions, chopped	¼ teaspoon cayenne (optional)
2 cloves garlic, pressed	1½ cups lentils
3 tomatoes, chopped	5½ cups water
1½ tablespoons curry powder	2 tablespoons low-sodium soy sauce

Place ½ cup water in a large saucepan. Add the onion and garlic, then cook, stirring frequently until softened, about 5 minutes. Add the tomatoes, curry powder, and cayenne. Continue to cook until the tomato softens, about 5 more minutes. Add the remaining water, lentils, and soy sauce. Bring to a boil, reduce the heat, cover, and cook for 30 minutes. Uncover and cook for an additional 45 minutes, stirring often because the filling will thicken.

To serve hot, fill chapatis, pita bread, or corn tortillas with some of the mixture. Garnish with chopped tomatoes, green onions, cucumber, fresh cilantro, and your favorite salsa.

BOSTON BAKED BEANS

Servings: 4-6 Preparation Time: 15 minutes
Cooking Time: 20 minutes

A sweet and sour baked bean dish that is an instant favorite. Preparation is fast because cooked beans are used.

1 medium onion, chopped

1 (16-ounce) can tomatoes, chopped

2 tablespoons maple syrup

1 tablespoon vinegar

1 tablespoon low-sodium soy sauce

1 tablespoon parsley flakes

1½ teaspoons dry mustard

1¼ teaspoons powdered ginger

½ teaspoon ground cinnamon

¼ teaspoon black pepper

5 cups white beans, cooked

Sauté the onion in a small amount of water until soft. Add the remaining ingredients, except for the beans. Cook and stir about 5 minutes. Add the beans, and cook about 10-15 minutes to blend flavors.

SIX-WAY-FUN CHILI

Servings: 8 Preparation Time: 45 minutes
Cooking Time: 3-4 hours

So named because of the six different toppings that are spooned over the top of the chili. You could make and serve it without the toppings, but it would be six times less fun. This recipe can also be made in a slow cooker. Just add all chili ingredients at once, and cook on high for 6-8 hours. Try serving over rice or another grain.

6 cups water	1½ tablespoons chili powder
2½ cups dried kidney beans	1 teaspoon cumin
4 onions, chopped	1 teaspoon carob powder
1 green pepper, chopped	¼ teaspoon cinnamon
2 stalks celery, sliced	¼ teaspoon ground coriander
1 (16-ounce) can tomatoes with juice, chopped	¼ teaspoon ground mustard
1 (6-ounce) can tomato paste	¼ teaspoon ground cardamom

Place the water and the beans in a large stockpot. Soak overnight (or bring to boil, boil 1 minute, remove from the heat and let rest 1 hour). Bring the beans and water to a boil again. Cook for 1 hour, then add the onions, green pepper, celery, tomatoes, and tomato paste. Stir to mix well. Cover and continue to cook over medium-low heat for 15 minutes. Then stir in spices. Cover and continue to cook until the beans are tender, 2 to 3 hours. Serve in large bowls.

Place the following six toppings in individual serving dishes. Pass these at the table to layer on the chili in any order desired.

CHILI TOPPINGS

Green Onions

1 bunch green onions, including tops, finely chopped

Tomatoes

2-3 tomatoes, chopped

Green Chilies

1 can diced green chilies

Cucumber

1 cucumber, peeled and chopped

Marinated Onions

1½ tablespoons vinegar

1 large red onion, sliced

2 teaspoons vinegar

1 tablespoon water

½ teaspoon mustard seeds

½ teaspoon cumin seeds

Place 2 cups water and 1½ tablespoon vinegar in a saucepan. Bring to a boil. Add the onions, cook 2 minutes, drain. Combine with the remaining ingredients. Refrigerate to blend flavors.

Greens

1 onion, chopped

10 cups finely chopped leafy greens
(2 bunches)

Sauté onion and greens in a small amount of water for a few minutes. Then cover and steam for about 10-15 minutes. Drain.

FEJOIADA

Servings: 6-8 Preparation Time: 1½ hours
Cooking Time: 3 hours

This is a traditional Brazilian dish. John's parents spent a year in Brazil in 1982. To everyone's delight, after their return I made this healthy version of a recipe that usually has meat toppings.

Beans

2½ cups dried black beans

5 cups water

1 large onion, chopped

2 stalks celery, chopped

2 cloves garlic, pressed

1 bay leaf

½ teaspoon crushed red pepper

2 medium tomatoes, chopped

Rice

2½ cups uncooked brown rice

3 cups water

2 cups tomato juice

Onions

2 onions, thinly sliced

2 tablespoons lemon juice

½ teaspoon Tabasco™ sauce

Greens

1 onion, chopped

10 cups finely chopped greens, about 2 large bunches greens (collards, Kale, romaine, chard, etc.)

Salsa

1 (16-ounce) can tomatoes, drained

¼ cup canned green chilies

½ small onion, chopped

2 tablespoons vinegar

1 tablespoon lemon juice

¼ teaspoon Tabasco™ sauce

Garnish

Peeled, sliced oranges

Place the beans and the water in a large pot. Soak overnight (or bring to a boil, boil 1 minute, remove from heat and let rest for 1 hour). Then bring to a boil, reduce the heat, cover, and simmer for 1 hour.

Add the onions, celery, garlic, bay leaf and crushed pepper. Continue to cook until the beans are almost tender, about 1½ hours. Add the tomatoes and cook an additional ½ hour.

Begin cooking the rice about 1 hour before dinner. Place water and juice in a saucepan. Bring to a boil. Add the rice, cover and simmer over low heat for 45 minutes. Remove from heat and let rest for 15 minutes before serving.

While the beans are cooking, place the onions in a saucepan with about ½ cup water. Sauté over medium heat until limp. Transfer to a bowl. Add the lemon juice and Tabasco. Mix well. Cover and refrigerate at least 1 hour to blend flavors.

Rinse the greens and drain. Finely chop the greens and the onion (use a food processor if you have one). Reserve the greens in a plastic bag until just before serving.

Place a small amount of water in a pan, add the greens and onion, and sauté until just wilted. Cover and steam about 10 minutes. Drain. Place in a serving bowl. Sprinkle with some fresh lemon juice.

To prepare the salsa, place all the ingredients in a blender jar. Blend until smooth. Refrigerate until serving time.

When ready to serve, place all ingredients in serving bowls. To assemble, place rice on plate first, cover with the black beans, then layer on the orange slices, the greens, the spicy onions and the salsa. Each person can add as much or as little of the extras as they wish.

Flavorful "Refried" Beans

Servings: 8-12   Preparation Time: 5 minutes
Cooking Time: 20 minutes

Everyone in our family agrees on this one—these beans are our favorite filling for burritos. The salsa really makes them special, so be sure to choose a salsa you love.

6 cups pinto beans, cooked	½ teaspoon onion powder
½ to 1 cup bean cooking liquid (or water)	½ teaspoon chili powder
½ teaspoon ground cumin	½ cup picante sauce or mild salsa

Mash the cooked pinto beans with a small amount of the cooking liquid (or water). Add cumin, onion powder, and chili powder. Stir in the salsa of your choice, either mild or spicy. Cook over low heat until heated through. Serve on tostados, chapatis, in pita bread, or in bean enchiladas.

SPICY CHINESE RICE

Servings: 6 Preparation Time: 30 minutes
Cooking Time: 20 minutes

My favorite rice dish, this is like a "fried" rice with the zest of extra spice and vegetables.

4 tablespoons low-sodium soy sauce

2 tablespoons cider vinegar

2 cloves garlic, crushed

2 teaspoons fresh ginger root, grated

¼ teaspoon crushed red pepper

1 onion, cut in half and sliced

½ pound mushrooms, sliced

1½ cups broccoli, chopped

2 cups Chinese cabbage, chopped

1 cup bean sprouts

2 cups optional sliced vegetable (asparagus, snow peas, celery, carrots, green onions, etc.)

4 cups cooked brown rice

1 tablespoon low-sodium soy sauce (optional)

3-4 tablespoons fresh cilantro, chopped

Place the soy sauce, cider vinegar, garlic, ginger root and crushed red pepper in a wok or large pot. Bring to a boil. Add the vegetables in batches so that each vegetable becomes coated with liquid, and cook and stir over medium-high heat until crisp-tender (about 10-15 minutes, depending on the size of the vegetable pieces). Begin with the onions and mushrooms, cook and stir for a minute, add the broccoli and optional vegetables, cook for a minute, then add the remaining vegetables and proceed as directed.

Add the cooked rice, the soy sauce, and the cilantro. Cook and stir until heated through. Serve at once.

Helpful Hints: This can easily be made in small amounts to serve less people. It keeps well for up to three days and can even be frozen. Other combinations of vegetables can also be used. Keep the pieces small so they cook quickly.

LASAGNA ROLL-UPS

Servings: 8-10 Preparation Time: 1½ hours
Cooking Time: 45 minutes

They're a lot of work, but the result is a meal you'll be proud to serve your most important guests. The use of tofu, which is high in fat, makes them extra rich and special.

Marinara Sauce *Yield: 8 cups*

1 yellow onion, finely chopped

½ pound fresh mushrooms, cleaned and finely chopped

2 cloves garlic, crushed

1 (15- to 16-ounce) can low-sodium stewed tomatoes

1 (15- to 16-ounce) can low-sodium tomato sauce

1 (15- to 16-ounce) can low-sodium tomato purée

1 teaspoon dried basil

1 teaspoon dried oregano

2 tablespoons parsley flakes

Sauté the onions, mushrooms and garlic in a small amount of water for 10 minutes. Add the remaining ingredients. Simmer, uncovered, over low heat 1-2 hours, until sauce thickens, breaking up the tomatoes as they cook.

Lasagna

20 spinach lasagna noodles

1 cup onions, chopped

2 pounds fresh spinach, chopped

2 cups tofu, mashed

¼ cup whole wheat flour

1 tablespoon low-sodium soy sauce

2 teaspoons oregano

½ teaspoon dill weed

1 teaspoon basil

Cook the lasagna noodles in boiling water until tender, about 8 minutes. Drain and set aside in cold water.

Wash the spinach, remove any tough stems, and chop. Set aside. Using a large pan, sauté the onion in ½ cup water until soft, about 5 minutes. Add the chopped spinach and sauté until limp. Add the tofu, soy sauce, oregano, basil, and dill weed. Mix well. Stir in ¼ cup whole wheat flour. Mix. Set aside.

Remove the lasagna noodles from the water and hang them over the edges of your sink to drain. Take the noodles, one at a time, and lay them flat. Spread about 2 tablespoons tofu mixture along the entire length of the noodle, then roll it up. Repeat until all the noodles are filled and rolled.

Place about 2 cups of the Marinara Sauce in the bottom of a large oblong baking dish (13" × 15").

Place the noodle roll-ups seam side down in the baking dish. Pour the remaining sauce over them. Cover. Bake at 350°F for 45 minutes.

Helpful Hints: This lasagna makes a wonderful meal for entertaining. It does take some extra time to prepare, but the result is worth it. If pressed for time, try substituting a 10-ounce package of frozen chopped spinach for the fresh spinach. Just thaw the frozen spinach in a colander, press out the excess water, and add it directly to the tofu mixture without steaming.

This mixture is also great for filling manicotti. Cover stuffed manicotti with Marinara Sauce, and bake as directed above. This recipe will fill 14 manicotti.

CHINESE NOODLES WITH VEGETABLES

Servings: 4 Preparation Time: 45 minutes
Cooking Time: 20 minutes

This recipe was developed during our Hawaiian days when I made lots of Oriental foods. If you enjoy Chinese foods, especially Chinese Vegetable Chow Mein, you'll love this. All the flavor remains, but the grease is gone.

1 pound whole wheat spaghetti or buckwheat soba noodles

4-6 dried mushrooms (shiitake)

6 green onions, chopped

1 teaspoon fresh ginger, grated

2 cups vegetables, thinly sliced

2 tablespoons low-sodium soy sauce

1 tablespoon sherry or rice vinegar

1 cup mushroom stock

Place about 6 cups of water in large pan. Heat to boiling. Add the noodles. Reduce the heat to medium low. Stir to separate the noodles. Cover. Simmer 10 minutes. Drain, rinse well, and chill.

Place the mushrooms in a bowl. Pour 1 cup of boiling water over them. Soak them for 15 minutes, then squeeze to remove excess water. Reserve the mushroom water.

Cut off the stems and discard. Cut the mushrooms into strips. Set aside.

In a wok or large pan, heat ¼ cup water. Add the green onions and grated ginger. Sauté for 1 minute.

Add mushrooms and vegetables. Cook and stir for 5 minutes.

Add the cooked noodles. Cook and stir 2 minutes longer.

Add the reserved mushroom stock, the soy sauce, and the sherry or vinegar. Mix well. Bring to a boil. Reduce the heat, cover and cook over medium heat 5 to 10 minutes, until the liquid is absorbed. Serve either hot or cold.

Helpful Hints: Some good vegetables to use are celery, carrots, green beans, asparagus, snow peas, Chinese cabbage, and broccoli. Try using all one vegetable, or combinations such as celery and carrots, asparagus and snow peas, snow peas and Chinese cabbage.

LAYERED RICE CASSEROLE

Servings: 8 Preparation Time: 30 minutes
Cooking Time: 45 minutes

One of the first casserole dishes I made after we started eating healthy, this dish has remained one of our favorites since the mid '70s. You can make it ahead and store it in the refrigerator until dinner time, so you're free to attend to other things before dinner.

5 cups cooked brown rice

1 cup cooked white beans

2 cups frozen corn kernels

2 cups canned tomatoes, broken up

1 onion, chopped

2 cloves garlic, crushed

1 tablespoon low-sodium soy sauce

1 teaspoon thyme

6 ounces tomato paste

½ cup water

paprika

Sauté the onion and garlic in ¼ cup water. Combine with the cooked beans, corn, tomatoes, soy sauce, and thyme. Combine the tomato paste and ½ cup water. In a casserole dish, layer 2½ cups cooked rice on the bottom, then the cooked bean vegetable mixture, then the tomato paste mixture. Cover with the remaining 2½ cups of cooked rice. Sprinkle with paprika. Bake at 350°F covered for 30 minutes, then uncovered for an additional 15 minutes.

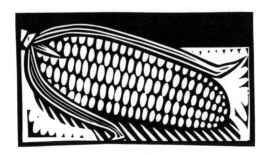

BARBEQUED BEANS

Servings: 6 Preparation Time: 15 minutes
Cooking Time: 20 minutes

These beans are great on a whole wheat bun (like a Sloppy Joe mix) with some acceptable ketchup and mustard, or served over whole grains. Delicious either hot or cold, they are good as a take-along for picnics or as a sandwich spread.

1 onion, chopped	½ teaspoon turmeric
1 green pepper, chopped	1 cup tomato sauce
1 clove garlic, crushed	1½ tablespoons unsulphured molasses
1½ teaspoons dry mustard	½ tablespoon apple cider vinegar
1½ teaspoons chili powder	dash (or two) Tabasco™ sauce
½ teaspoon ground cumin	4 cups cooked beans (pink, kidney, red, or pinto)

Sauté the onion, green pepper, and garlic in ¼ cup water for 5 minutes. Add the mustard, chili powder, cumin, and turmeric. Stir to mix well. Add the remaining ingredients. Mix well. Cook over low heat until heated through, about 15 minutes.

SIMPLE SAUCES

BROWN GRAVY

Yield: 1½ quarts Preparation Time: 10 minutes
Cooking Time: 30 minutes

This is about as close as you're going to get to the taste of a beef gravy without the fleshy flavor. You'll find the transition to this gravy an easy one, especially when it's served over your family's favorite starch, like potatoes or rice. It's our boys' favorite gravy.

¼ cup water

1 onion, finely chopped

1 cup whole wheat pastry flour

5½ cups water

½ cup low-sodium soy sauce

Heat the water in a large saucepan over medium heat and sauté the onion for 5 minutes, until translucent. Blend in the flour and stir well. Cook for 3-4 minutes, until lightly browned. Add the water and soy sauce. Cook over medium heat, stirring often, until the sauce thickens. Add more water if too thick.

Helpful Hints: Sauté some chopped mushrooms with the onions. Use as a sauce for steamed vegetables, grains, potatoes, or a vegetable pie. Try steaming your favorite vegetables, serve with brown rice, and top with Brown Gravy.

If you prefer a smooth gravy (no onion or mushroom pieces), blend the gravy at high speed in the blender about halfway through the cooking time. Then return it to the pan and continue to cook and stir until thickened.

This gravy freezes well, and the recipe makes a large amount. Freeze some for later use or cut the recipe in half if you don't want so much.

MUSHROOM GRAVY

Yield: about 2½ cups   Preparation Time: 15 minutes
Cooking Time: 30 minutes

This is John's parents' and his sister's favorite. The spices are distinct, so you'll probably take an instant liking or dislike to it.

½ pound mushrooms, chopped

2 leeks, sliced

2¼ cups water

1 teaspoon oregano

1 teaspoon thyme

1 tablespoon low-sodium soy sauce

4 tablespoons arrowroot or cornstarch

Sauté the mushrooms and leeks with the oregano and thyme in ¼ cup water for 10 minutes. Mix the cornstarch or arrowroot and soy sauce with 2 cups of cold water. Add to the mushroom-leek mixture. Cook over low heat, stirring frequently, until it thickens (about 20 minutes).

Helpful Hints: Use 1 chopped onion if no leeks are available. Serve over rice or other grains, potatoes, griddle cakes, waffles, bean or grain loaves, burgers, or vegetables.

QUICK ENCHILADA SAUCE

Yield: 2½ cups Preparation Time: 5 minutes
Cooking Time: 10 minutes

This sauce is our daughter's favorite. We can't have a burrito meal when she's home without this sauce. Most Mexican food lovers will take to this sauce effortlessly.

1 cup tomato sauce

1½ cups water

⅛ teaspoon garlic powder

¼ teaspoon onion powder

1½ tablespoons chili powder blend

2 tablespoons cornstarch or arrowroot

Place all the ingredients in a saucepan. Mix well. Cook and stir over medium heat until the mixture boils and thickens, about 10 minutes.

Helpful Hints: Serve over bean burritos or chapatis and beans. Serve over grains or vegetables. Use to give any food a Mexican flavor.

GINGER SAUCE

Yield: about 2½ cups   Preparation Time: 15 minutes
Cooking Time: 10 minutes

This sauce has an Oriental flavor, but you don't have to serve it only with rice. It's delicious with potatoes, pasta, and corn.

¼ cup low-sodium soy sauce

2 cups water

2 tablespoons sherry (optional)

1½ tablespoons grated fresh ginger root

½ cup chopped green onions

1 clove garlic, crushed

4 tablespoons arrowroot or cornstarch mixed in ¼ cup water

Mix all ingredients together in a saucepan. Cook and stir over medium heat until thickened, about 10 minutes.

Helpful Hints: Serve over rice or noodles. Mix with steamed vegetables. This sauce will keep well in refrigerator for up to five days. Do not freeze.

SZECHUAN SAUCE

Yield: 2 cups Preparation Time: 10 minutes
Cooking Time: 10 minutes

This is a very spicy sauce. Use less Tabasco and less ginger if you prefer a milder one. It does wonders for steamed vegetables.

1¾ cups water

2 tablespoons low-sodium soy sauce

1 tablespoon cornstarch or arrowroot

1 tablespoon fresh ginger root, grated

2 green onions, finely chopped

½ teaspoon Tabasco™ sauce

Combine all ingredients in a saucepan. Cook and stir over medium heat until mixture boils and thickens, about 10 minutes. Serve over rice or other grains, or use as a topping for potatoes or pasta.

SIDE DISHES

UNFORGETTABLE CHINESE EGGPLANT

Servings: 6 Preparation Time: 15 minutes
Cooking Time: 20-25 minutes

The idea for this very spicy eggplant dish came from a favorite dish served in a hole-in-the-wall Chinese restaurant in downtown Honolulu. Once the oil was removed from this vegetarian selection, it became deliciously McDougall.

4 medium-long eggplants	2 stalks green onions
4 cloves garlic, crushed	2 tablespoons low-sodium soy sauce
1 thumb-size piece of ginger root	¼ teaspoon crushed red chili pepper (optional)

Cut the eggplants into ½" × 1" pieces. Cook in a small amount of boiling water until almost done (5-8 minutes). Drain.

Slice the ginger, garlic and green onions into ⅟₁₆-inch slivers. Sauté the ginger and garlic in 1 tablespoon water for about 2 minutes on high heat. Add the eggplant pieces and continue to cook for a few minutes. Add the soy sauce, green onions (and optional chili pepper, if desired). Cook until done, the softer the better.

Serve with brown rice.

BROILED DIJON TOMATOES

Servings: 4 Preparation Time: 10 minutes
Cooking Time: 3-4 minutes

We serve this in the McDougall Program at St. Helena Hospital, adding a special touch by sprinkling bread crumbs over the top.

4 tomatoes, cut in half

2 cloves garlic, pressed

1 tablespoon Dijon mustard

¼ teaspoon dry mustard

½ teaspoon water

In a small bowl, combine the garlic, Dijon mustard and dry mustard. Add the water, a little at a time, stirring as you do so. Put the tomatoes on a broiling pan and spread the mustard mixture over them. Broil the tomatoes under a preheated broiler (about 3 inches from heat) for 3-4 minutes until bubbly. Watch them carefully; they burn easily.

SAUTÉED MUSHROOMS

Servings: 2-4   Preparation Time: 10 minutes
Cooking Time: 10 minutes

Serve plain or as a topping for baked potatoes, acorn squash, or whole grains. Try making this recipe without the onions. Cut the mushrooms in half or leave them whole.

1 large onion, chopped or sliced

½ pound mushrooms, thickly sliced

½ cup white wine

2 cloves garlic, crushed

Place all ingredients in a saucepan. Sauté over medium heat about 10 minutes, until the mushrooms are tender but not mushy.

ZUCCHINI-CORN CASSEROLE

Servings: 6   Preparation Time: 20 minutes
Cooking Time: 30 minutes

A nice complement to a Mexican meal.

3-4 zucchini, sliced ¼ inch thick

2 cups frozen corn kernels

1 cup mild Mexican salsa

1 onion, sliced

Place ½ cup water in a large pot. Add the onion and sauté briefly. Add the zucchini, stir a few times, then cover and steam about 10 minutes. Remove from the heat. Mix in the corn kernels and salsa. Turn into a casserole dish, cover and bake at 400°F for 30 minutes.

CAJUN POTATOES

Servings: 4 Preparation Time: 10 minutes
Cooking Time: 20 minutes

If you like Cajun flavors, you'll find this spicy potato side dish a real treat.

2 pounds new potatoes

2 tablespoons Cajun Spices (see below)

3 cups water

Scrub the potatoes and leave whole. Place the potatoes, spices and water in a saucepan. Bring to a boil, cover and cook for 15-20 minutes or until the potatoes are tender. Be careful not to let them get mushy.

Helpful Hints: If you cannot find new potatoes, use white potatoes scrubbed and cut into chunks. Follow the same instructions as above. For a spicier version, remove the saucepan cover for the last 10 minutes of cooking and let some of the water evaporate.

CAJUN SPICES

Yield: ⅓ cup Preparation Time: 5 minutes
Cooking Time: none

Try this for an excellent spicy topping for popcorn, or use spices over potatoes, rice, corn or green and yellow vegetables. These spices are also used in the Cajun Bean Stew on page 93.

3 tablespoons paprika

2 teaspoons onion powder

2 teaspoons ground black pepper

2 teaspoons ground white pepper

2 teaspoons ground red pepper

1 teaspoon oregano

1 teaspoon thyme

½ teaspoon celery seed

Mix all ingredients and store in a tightly covered container.

CHINESE CABBAGE WITH BEAN SPROUTS

Servings: 6 Preparation Time: 15 minutes
Cooking Time: 15 minutes

A nice addition to an Oriental meal. Soy sauce sprinkled over the top at the table makes this dish special.

½ pound mushrooms, sliced

2 cloves garlic, minced

½ teaspoon fresh ginger root, grated

½ cup water

2 cups Chinese cabbage, shredded

2 cups bean sprouts

In a large pot, cook the mushrooms, garlic, and grated ginger in the water for 5 minutes. Add the remaining vegetables. Stir to mix well. Cover and steam about 10 minutes, stirring occasionally. Serve hot.

HERBED GREEN BEANS

Servings: 4 Preparation Time: 10 minutes
Cooking Time: 20 minutes

Fresh green beans go well with most everything. We enjoy them as a side dish with spaghetti and stews.

1 pound fresh green beans	1 teaspoon parsley flakes
½ teaspoon basil	1 teaspoon chives
½ teaspoon marjoram	⅛ teaspoon thyme
½ teaspoon chervil	⅛ teaspoon summer savory (optional)

Wash and trim the beans. Cut into 2-inch pieces. Place in a pot with a steamer basket and about 1 inch of water. Steam until crisp-tender, about 20 minutes. Combine the herbs in a small bowl. When the beans are done, drain off the water and place them in a serving bowl. Add the herb mixture, toss beans lightly to coat with the mixture. Serve at once.

DESSERTS

RICH MOIST FRUITCAKE

Yield: 1 loaf Preparation Time: 30 minutes
Cooking Time: 45 minutes

We've been teaching classes on health since the mid '70s. This recipe is always such a big hit we include it in every class. Many followers of our program choose this recipe over a birthday cake on that special day of the year.

1 cup carrots, grated	¼ teaspoon ground cloves
1 cup raisins	1¾ cups water
½ cup honey	1½ cups whole wheat flour
¼ cup dates, chopped	1 teaspoon baking soda
1 teaspoon cinnamon	½ cup bran
1 teaspoon allspice	½ cup walnuts, chopped (optional)
½ teaspoon nutmeg	

Cook the carrots, raisins, dates, honey, and spices in the water for 10 minutes. Cool. Mix together the flour, baking soda, bran, and walnuts. Add to the carrot mixture. Mix together well. Pour into a nonstick loaf pan or 9" × 9" baking dish. Bake at 325°F for 45 minutes.

Variations: Substitute grated zucchini or apple for the carrots. Substitute prunes or figs for the raisins, or use all dates.

LITTLE KITCHEN APPLE-RAISIN BARS

Yield: one 9" × 13" pan   Preparation Time: 60 minutes
Cooking Time: 45 minutes

The Little Kitchen was a small restaurant in a health food store in Kailua, Hawaii. People would come in for lunch just to have one of these bars.

Crust

1¼ cups whole wheat pastry flour

2 cups rolled oats

6 tablespoons sesame seeds

5 ounces unsweetened applesauce

½ cup honey

¾ cup water

½ cup raw almonds, chopped

Filling

peel from ½ an orange

peel from ¼ a lemon

2 oranges

2 cups dried apples, cut in small pieces

1 cup raisins

1 cup apple juice

2 teaspoons vanilla

Crust: Combine all crust ingredients except for almonds. Mix well. Set aside.

Filling: Cut orange peel and lemon peel in pieces and mince in food processor or blender. Peel the oranges, cut them in chunks and process with the fruit peels. Put this mixture in a saucepan with all the other filling ingredients and cook over low heat until very soft. (Add a little water while cooking, if necessary, to prevent sticking.)

To assemble: Use a 9" × 13" nonstick baking pan (if you do not have a nonstick pan, you will need to lightly oil and flour your pan). Take ⅔ of the crust mixture and press it into the bottom of the pan. Spread the filling mix over the crust. Add the chopped almonds to the remaining ⅓ of the crust mixture and mix well. Sprinkle this on top of the fruit mixture and press down to form the top crust. Bake at 375°F for 35 minutes. Turn the pan around and bake for 10 minutes more.

Let cool before slicing into bars. Makes 30 bars (1" × 2").

Helpful Hints: To make date bars, replace the apples and raisins with 3 cups of date pieces.

TOFU CHEESECAKE

Servings: 8-10 Preparation Time: 45 minutes
Chilling Time: at least 1 hour

This recipe tastes so rich, you won't believe it's a McDougall creation. But don't forget, tofu is 54% fat, and this recipe is almost all tofu.

Crust

2 cups Grape Nuts cereal or oil-free granola

⅓ cup apple juice concentrate, thawed

Topping

3 tablespoons grated carob chips

Filling

2 cubes tofu (16 ounces each, firm if possible)

¾ cup honey

1 tablespoon carob powder

1 teaspoon vanilla

¼ teaspoon cinnamon

Break up the Grape Nuts or granola in a blender or with a rolling pin. Place in a bowl. Add the apple juice concentrate and mix well. Press into a 9" or 9½" pie pan. Combine the tofu and honey. Mix well. Add the remaining ingredients and beat with an electric beater until fluffy. Spoon filling into the cereal crust. Sprinkle grated carob chips over the filling. Chill for at least 1 hour before serving.

Helpful Hints: If the tofu is not firm, wrap it in a towel and place it in the refrigerator for about an hour to remove the excess water. The longer the cheesecake chills after making, the firmer it will become and the richer it will taste. Try to prepare it 6-8 hours before serving for best results. Cover the cheesecake loosely with plastic wrap while chilling.

APRICOT TOFU PIE

Yield: 1 pie Preparation Time: 60 minutes
Cooking Time: none

I made this pie once for a TV show called International Kitchen. After the show, the TV crew make short work of the pie! They were amazed how rich and delicious a dessert made of tofu could taste.

Crust

2 cups Grape Nuts cereal

⅓ cup apple juice concentrate, thawed

Filling

¼ cup agar-agar flakes

6 ounces dried apricots

½ cup honey

1 teaspoon vanilla

1 (20-ounce) package firm tofu

Break up the Grape Nuts in a blender and place in a bowl. Add the apple juice concentrate and mix well. Press into a springform pan or a 9" pie pan.

In a small saucepan, sprinkle the agar-agar flakes over 1 cup of water and set aside to soften. In another saucepan, bring the apricots to a boil in 1½ cups water. Cook until soft, but not mushy. Remove 9 apricot halves to use later as garnish. Cook the remaining apricots until no water remains in the pan. Put them in a blender or food processor and blend well. Cut the tofu into chunks and process it with the apricots until the mixture is very smooth. Add the honey to the agar-water mixture and bring it to a boil for a few minutes until the agar dissolves. Add the vanilla. With the food processor running, pour the agar mixture into the apricot-tofu mixture. Blend well, then pour immediately into the pie crust. Refrigerate until set. (This usually sets up in about 15 minutes.) Put one apricot half in the center of the pie and arrange the other eight around the center one.

CAROB FRUIT FONDUE

Yield: 1 cup sauce Servings: 2 people (with fruit)
Preparation Time: 5 minutes Cooking Time: 10 minutes

This is a low-fat, fun dessert. Just like chocolate fondue (but without guilt), you can have the after-dinner ritual of serving yourself with fondue spears—dipping fruit into an "almost chocolate" sauce you may find even tastier than the original stuff.

1 tablespoon roasted carob power	1 (6-ounce) can apple juice concentrate, thawed
2 teaspoons cornstarch or arrowroot	1 teaspoon vanilla
2 tablespoons water	2 cups mixed fresh fruit, cut in chunks

Combine the carob powder and cornstarch or arrowroot in a small saucepan. Gradually add the water to make a smooth paste. Stir in the apple juice concentrate. Cook over low heat, stirring constantly until thickened. Stir in the vanilla. Place sauce in a fondue pot or chafing dish to keep warm for dipping. Dip pieces of fresh fruit into warm sauce. Try chunks of bananas, apples, pineapple, honeydew melon, or cantaloupe.

Helpful Hints: Substitute unsweetened orange or pineapple juice for the apple juice.

MOM'S BANANA BREAD

Yield: 1 loaf Preparation Time: 15 minutes
Cooking Time: 60 minutes

John grew up with this recipe. After his parents learned to eat healthier, his mother made a few modifications that left the taste intact and eliminated the fat.

2¼ cups whole wheat flour

1 teaspoon baking soda

1 teaspoon baking powder

1 (12-ounce) can frozen apple juice concentrate

4 ripe bananas

3 teaspoons egg replacer mixed with 6 tablespoons water

Mix the dry ingredients together. Mash the bananas, and mix them with the apple juice concentrate, egg replacer and water. Combine the wet and dry ingredients and beat with a whisk or electric mixer. Pour into a lightly oiled or nonstick loaf pan. Bake at 350°F for 60 minutes.

CARROT CAKE

Yield : one 13" × 9" cake Preparation Time: 40 minutes
Cooking Time: 1 hour

This is a traditional carrot cake with lots of moisture, but no fat or eggs. No doubt about it—unless you don't like sweets, you'll love this.

2 cups whole wheat flour	½ teaspoon nutmeg
¾ cups honey	½ teaspoon cloves
1¼ cups applesauce	½ teaspoon allspice
4 teaspoons egg replacer, well mixed in 8 table-spoons water	3 cups grated carrots
1½ teaspoons baking soda	1 (8-ounce) can pineapple, crushed (slightly drained)
2 teaspoons baking powder	½ cup raisins
2 teaspoons cinnamon	1 cup chopped walnuts (optional)

Mix the dry ingredients together (flour, spices, baking soda, and powder).

Add the honey, applesauce, and mixed egg replacer. Mix well.

Add carrots, pineapple, raisins, and nuts. Stir well.

Turn into a nonstick baking pan 13" × 9" × 2". Bake at 350°F for 1 hour.

Helpful Hints: If you do not have a nonstick baking pan, you will have to lightly oil and flour your pan.

POACHED PEARS

Servings: 6 Preparation Time: 45 minutes
Cooking Time: 30 minutes Chilling Time: 2 hours

Originally designed by the chef at the Outrigger Canoe Club in Honolulu, this makes a beautiful, elegant dessert, well worth your efforts for a celebration meal.

Pears

6 pears, pared

2 cups chablis

2 cups water

1 cinnamon stick

2 cloves

1½ cups honey

zest and juice of ½ orange

zest and juice of ½ lemon

Pare pears. Bring the other ingredients to a boil in a large saucepan. Add the pears. Poach about 30 minutes, or until tender. To test, pierce with a skewer or a fork. Cool pears in the liquid, then remove from liquid and chill.

Sauce

1 pound fresh strawberries, cleaned

6 tablespoons honey

1 tablespoon fresh orange juice

small amount water as needed

Place all ingredients in a blender and purée.
Place a pear on an individual serving plate. Pour a little sauce over pear. Garnish with orange segments and mint leaves. Repeat with all pears.
Helpful Hints: Apple juice may be substituted for the chablis.

ALPHABETICAL INDEX

M

Manhattan Bean Soup, 40
Marinated Mushrooms, 27
Mediterranean Mushrooms, 78
Mexican Bean Soup, 41
Mild Gazpacho, 35
Mom's Banana Bread, 126
Mu Shu Tofu, 62
Mushroom Gravy, 109
Mushroom Soup, 47

O

Oriental Vegetable Soup, 31

P

Pasta Salad Bowl, 57
Peasant's Pie, 73
Poached Pears, 128
Polynesian Vegetables, 76
Potato Chowder, 49
Potato Pancakes, 68

Q

Quick Confetti Rice, 72
Quick Enchilada Sauce, 110
Quick Vegetable Stew, 77

R

Rice Summer Salad, 52
Rich Moist Fruitcake, 121

S

Sautéed Mushrooms, 116
Shish-Kebabs, 65
Six-Way-Fun Chili, 96
South of the Border Soup, 46

Spaghetti Sauce, 80
Spaghetti Squash Surprise, 61
Spanish Garbanzo Soup, 43
Spanish Rice, 82
Spicy Chinese Rice, 101
Spicy Lentil Filling, 94
Stove Top Stew, 88
Stuffed Cabbage Rolls, 85
Stuffed Mushroom Caps, 29
Stuffed Peppers, 70
Stuffed Pumpkin, 60
Summer Vegetable Delight, 92
Summertime Chowder, 38
Super Sprout Salad, 56
Szechuan Sauce, 112

T

Tabouli, 51
Tamale Pie, 69
Three Bean Salad, 58
Tofu Cheesecake, 123
Tossed Green Rice, 83

U

Unforgettable Chinese Eggplant,
114

V

Vegetable Chop Suey, 63
Vegetable Stuffed Peppers with
Spicy Tomato Sauce, 86

W

White Bean Soup, 34
White Mushroom Sauce, 81
Wicked Mushrooms, 79

Z
Zucchini-Corn Casserole, 116

SUBJECT INDEX